NATIONAL GEOGRAPHIC
KIDS

Just Joking

300
hilarious jokes,
tricky
tongue twisters,
and ridiculous
riddles

NATIONAL
GEOGRAPHIC
WASHINGTON, D.C.

Lions rest for about 20 hours a day.

4

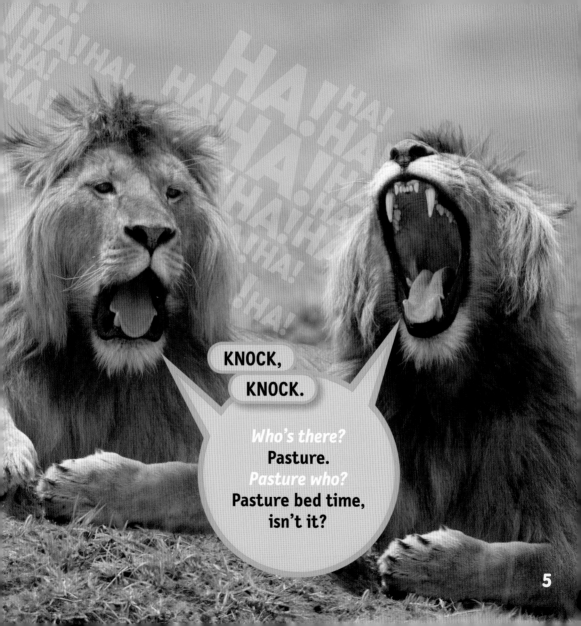

5

A sea otter's fur helps it float by trapping air inside the strands.

KNOCK, KNOCK.

Who's there?
Lena.
Lena who?
Lena little closer and I'll tell you.

6

Q How are **two banana peels** like shoes?

A They're a pair of slippers.

7

Shoes are required
to eat in the cafeteria.
Socks can eat
anyplace they want.

Q What do you call a shy lamb?

A *Baaash-ful.*

Q Why did cavemen draw pictures of hippopotamuses and rhinoceroses on their wall?

A *Because they couldn't spell the animals' names.*

Q On what **nuts** can pictures hang?

A *Wall-nuts.*

8

A Reinwardt's flying frog has webbed feet to help it glide down from the treetops.

9

Grizzly bears can run up to 30 miles an hour (48 kph).

10

11

Q What happened when 500 hares got loose in the center of town?

A The police had to comb the area.

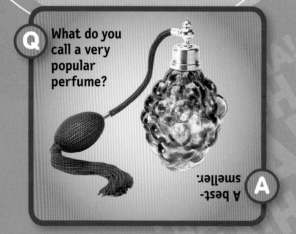

Q What do you call a very popular perfume?

A A best-smeller.

12

The American alligator species is more than 150 million years old.

KNOCK, KNOCK.

Who's there?
Nuisance.
Nuisance who?
What's nuisance yesterday?

A polar bear has rough paw pads to keep it from slipping on the ice.

What do you call a **polar bear** wearing earmuffs?

Anything you want. He can't hear you!

TONGUE TWISTER!

Say this fast three times:

Dracula digs dreary, dark dungeons.

Q What happens when a ghost gets lost in the fog?

A He is mist.

Q What do you call two spiders that just got married?

A Newlywebs.

Q What paces back and forth on the ocean floor?

A A nervous wreck.

15

Cooks cook cup

cakes quickly.

A female lion usually gives birth to three to five lion cubs at a time.

KNOCK, KNOCK.

Who's there?
Cash.
Cash who?
No, thanks. I prefer peanuts.

Q What goes *thump, thump, thump,* **squish,** *thump, thump, thump,* **squish?**

A An elephant with one wet shoe.

TONGUE TWISTER!

Say this fast three times:

Jolly juggling jesters juggle jingle jacks.

Q What kind of fish goes best with peanut butter?

A Jellyfish.

Q When is a baseball player like a spider?

A When he catches a fly.

Q What did the beach say when the tide came in?

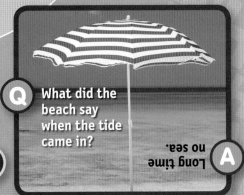

A Long time no sea.

KNOCK, KNOCK.

Who's there?
Hugo.
Hugo who?
Hugo-ing to let me in or not?

About 99 percent of a red panda's diet is bamboo.

21

Bulldogs can weigh as much as 50 pounds—that's more than three bowling balls.

22

23

Bottlenose dolphins have little or no sense of smell.

KNOCK, KNOCK.

Who's there?
Kent.
Kent who?
Kent you tell who it is?

24

Q What did the chewing gum say to the shoe?

A I'm stuck on you.

Q What goes **zzub zzub?**

A A bee flying backward.

TONGUE TWISTER!

Say this fast three times:

Quick kiss, quicker kiss.

Q What is in an astronaut's favorite sandwich?

A Launch meat.

25

CUSTOMER:
Do you serve crabs?

WAITRESS:
Of course, sir. We serve anyone.

Q Did you just **pick** your nose?

A No, I've had it since I was born.

Q What has a big **mouth** and doesn't say a word?

A A river.

Q Why does it get hot after a baseball game?

A Because all the fans have left.

26

Fishers are mammals found only in northern North America.

KNOCK, KNOCK.

Who's there?
Ben.
Ben who?
Ben knocking on the door all afternoon.

27

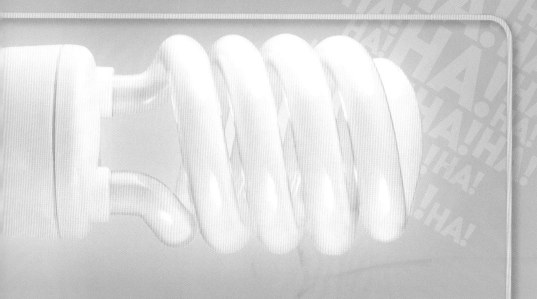

HA!HA!
HA!HA!HA!
HA!HA!HA!
HA!HA!HA!
HA!HA!

Why did the robot eat a lightbulb?

Because he was in need of a light snack.

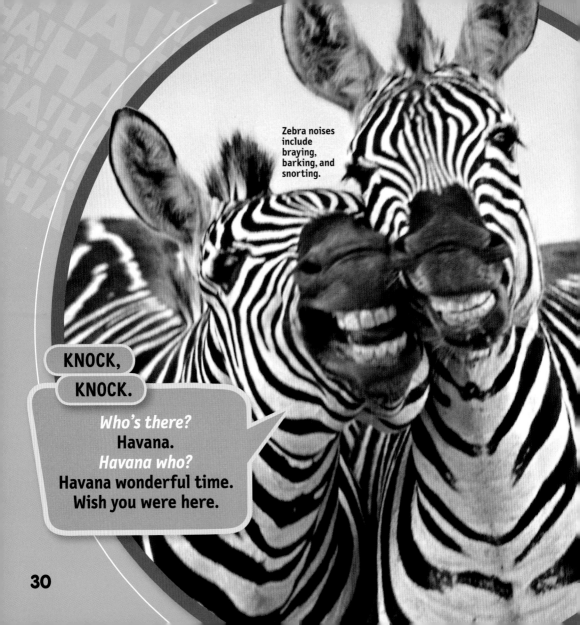

Zebra noises include braying, barking, and snorting.

KNOCK, KNOCK.

Who's there?
Havana.
Havana who?
Havana wonderful time. Wish you were here.

Q What do **planets** use to download **music?**

A Neptunes.

Q Why does Santa have three gardens?

A So he can hoe, hoe, hoe!

Q Why are grapes never alone?

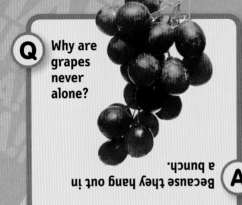

A Because they hang out in a bunch.

Q How do **bees** get to **school?**

A On the school buzz.

TONGUE TWISTER!

Say this fast three times:

A moose noshes much mush.

Q What do you call a **COW** that doesn't give milk?

A A milk dud.

KNOCK,
KNOCK.

Who's there?
Olive.
Olive who?
Olive you!

The word "hamster" comes from the German word *hamstern*, meaning to hoard.

33

34

The Roseate spoonbill's wingspan is more than four feet (1.2 m) wide.

35

What protects a
clown
from the sun?

The bozone layer.

Q What did the **Atlantic Ocean** say to the **Pacific Ocean?**

A Nothing. It just waved.

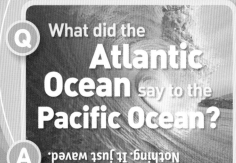

Q What do anteaters have that other animals don't have?

A Baby anteaters.

Say this fast three times:

Comical cactus curls rural wind.

Q

What did one **math book** say to the other math book?

A I've got a lot of problems.

Q What happened to the frog that parked illegally?

A He was toad away.

Q What asks no questions but must be answered?

A The doorbell.

A baby orca, or calf, is usually born tail-first.

39

Patty picks pretty

paper packages.

What two things can you not have for breakfast?

Lunch and dinner.

42

Q What do planets **read?**

A Comet books.

Q What do you call a freight train loaded with bubble gum?

A A chew-chew train.

DOCTOR: You need new glasses.
PATIENT: How do you know? I haven't told you what's wrong with me yet.
DOCTOR: I could tell as soon as you walked in through the window.

Arctic ground squirrels hibernate seven months out of the year.

KNOCK, KNOCK.

Who's there?
Huron.
Huron who?
Huron my toe. Could you please get off it?

44

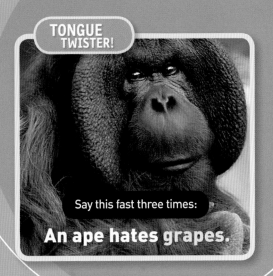

TONGUE TWISTER!

Say this fast three times:

An ape hates grapes.

Q What has **two legs** but can't walk?

A pair of pants. **A**

46

There are 17 species of macaws, including this military macaw.

TONGUE TWISTER!

Say this fast three times:

A tiny tiger thinks tough thoughts.

What do cows and dogs have in common? Q

A **They both like classical music. Moo-zart and Wag-ner.**

Q

How do you turn soup into gold?

Add 24 carrots.

A

Q **If chickens wake up when the rooster crows, when do ducks wake up?**

At the quack of dawn. A

Why did **Dracula** become a **vegetarian?**

Because his doctor told him "stake" was bad for his heart.

Sea otters use their stomachs as tables while they snack.

KNOCK, KNOCK.

Who's there?
Annie.
Annie who?
Annie body home?

50

Q Why did the **cat** put an **M** into the **freezer?**

A It turns into mice.

TONGUE TWISTER!

Say this fast three times:

Brenda's bunny baked buttered bread.

Q Why did the chicken cross the dusty road twice?

A Because she was a dirty double-crosser.

Q What do you call a nervous zucchini?

A An edgy veggie.

Like most parrots, Budgerigar parakeets have two toes facing forward and two facing back.

What do you get when you cross a **parakeet** with a a lawn mower?

Shredded tweet!

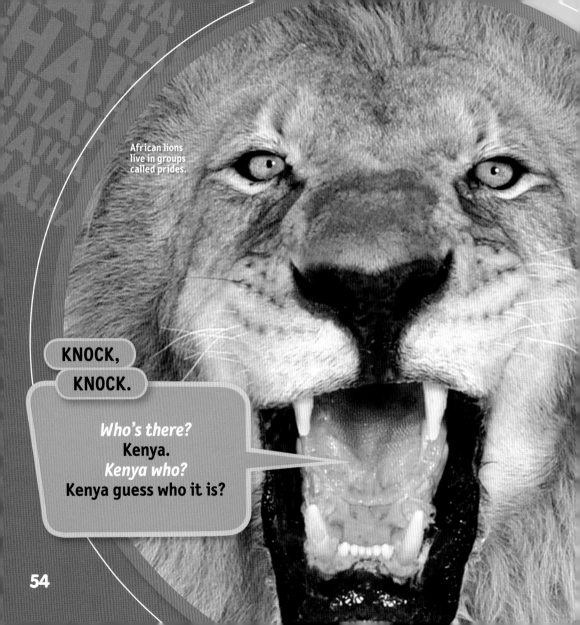

African lions live in groups called prides.

KNOCK, KNOCK.

Who's there?
Kenya.
Kenya who?
Kenya guess who it is?

54

Say this fast three times:

Speak sphinx.

Q How is baseball like cake?

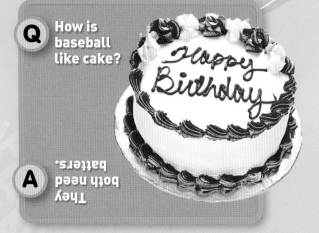

A They both need batters.

MOTHER: Jay, let your brother have the sled half the time!

JAY: I do, Mom. I have it going downhill and he has it going up.

Q

What do George **Washington,** Christopher **Columbus,** and Abraham **Lincoln** have in common?

A They were all born on a holiday!

Q

What can hold a **car** but can't lift a feather?

A A garage.

Q How do baby birds learn how to fly?

A They wing it.

TOURIST: How would you describe the **rain** in this part of the country?

LOCAL: Little drops of water falling from the sky.

KNOCK,
KNOCK.

Who's there?
Distressing.
Distressing who?
Distressing has too
much vinegar!

58

A crocodile's eyes and nostrils are on top of its head so it can see and breathe when lying just below the water's surface.

KNOCK, KNOCK.

Who's there?
Scold.
Scold who?
Scold out here!

Gentoo penguins are the fastest diving birds in the world.

TONGUE TWISTER!

Say this fast three times:

Many an anemone sees an enemy anemone.

Q What travels around the world but never leaves its corner?

A A postage stamp.

Q

What do you get when you cross a **turkey** with a **centipede?**

A Drumsticks for everyone.

Q Why are dolphins more clever than humans?

A Dolphins can train people to feed them fish.

Q What is the best way to keep dogs out of the street?

A Put them in a barking lot.

TONGUE TWISTER!

Say this fast three times:

Sly Sam slurps Sally's soup.

62

Tegus are large carnivorous lizards that grow up to 4 feet long (1.2 m).

KNOCK, KNOCK.

Who's there?
Woo.
Woo who?
Don't get so excited—it's just a joke.

63

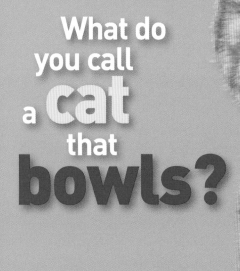

What do
you call
a **cat**
that
bowls?

An alley cat.

Roughly 30
percent of
households in the
United States own
at least one cat.

Elephant seals live in both extremely cold and extremely warm places, including Antarctica and Mexico.

66

TONGUE TWISTER!

Say this fast three times:

See Shep slip.

What do you get when you cross a bear with a skunk? **Q**

A Winnie the phew.

67

Say this fast three times:

Are our oars oak?

Q What is a monster's favorite place to swim?

A Lake Erie.

Q What do you call the mushy stuff between a shark's teeth?

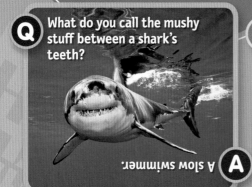

A A slow swimmer.

Q How does a mouse feel after a bath?

A Squeaky clean.

Where do smart **hot dogs** end up?

On the honor roll.

The Asian elephant uses a fingerlike feature on the end of its trunk to grab small items.

KNOCK, KNOCK.

Who's there?
Howl.
Howl who?
Howl I get in if you don't open the door?

70

71

KNOCK, KNOCK.

Who's there?
Waddle.
Waddle who?
Waddle I do if you don't open the door?

Like all ducks, this Pekin duck's feet have no blood vessels or nerves, so its feet never get cold.

72

Q Why did the farmer plow his field with a steamroller?

A Because he wanted mashed potatoes.

Q What do you get when you **cross a pig** with a **centipede?**

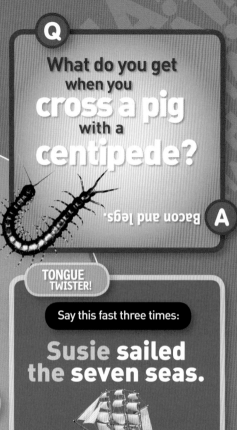

A Bacon and legs.

TONGUE TWISTER!

Say this fast three times:

Susie sailed the seven seas.

Q How do you communicate with a fish?

A Drop it a line.

Q What **nails** do carpenters hate to hit?

A Fingernails.

TONGUE TWISTER!

Say this fast three times:

Which wristwatch is a Swiss wristwatch?

Q What did the cheeseburger name its daughter?

A Patty.

74

TONGUE TWISTER!

Say this fast three times:

Ten tricky two-toed turkeys trotted.

She freed

six sheep.

Sheep travel in flocks to protect themselves from predators.

A serval can leap ten feet in the air and change direction mid-leap.

KNOCK, KNOCK.

Who's there?
Cook.
Cook who?
Hey! Who are you calling a cuckoo?

Q Why did the crook take a bath before he robbed the bank?

A So he could make a clean getaway.

TONGUE TWISTER!

Say this fast three times:

She shouldn't shake the salt shakers, should she?

TEACHER: Why does the Statue of Liberty stand in New York harbor?

STUDENT: Because it can't sit down.

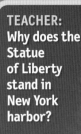

Q How do you fix a broken jack-o'-lantern?

A With a pumpkin patch.

Q What is at the **end** of everything?

A The letter g.

TONGUE TWISTER!

Say this fast three times:

6 silly **sisters** sort short **socks.**

Bare-backed
fruit bats live in
Australia,
Indonesia, Papua
New Guinea, and
East Timor.

81

Dromedary camels have one hump; Bactrian camels, like this one, have two.

KNOCK, KNOCK.

Who's there?
Snow.
Snow who?
Snow time for questions. Just let me in!

A green tree frog's call sounds like "quonk, quonk, quonk."

KNOCK, KNOCK.

Who's there?
Twig.
Twig who?
Twig or treat!

What has a **bottom** at the top?

A Your legs!

Q Why do birds fly south for the winter?

A It's easier than walking.

Q Which weighs more, a ton of feathers or a ton of bricks?

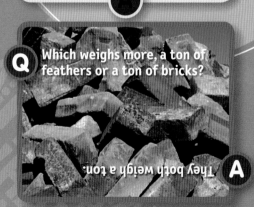

A They both weigh a ton.

Q What did one **ghost** say to the other ghost?

A "Get a life!"

85

Q

How do fleas travel from place to place?

A They itch-hike.

Q When do you go at red and stop at green?

A When you're eating watermelon.

86

This Asian elephant has smaller, rounder ears than an African elephant.

KNOCK, KNOCK.

Who's there?
Figs.
Figs who?
Figs the doorbell—it's broken!

What would you get if you crossed a jazz musician with a sweet potato?

Yam sessions.

89

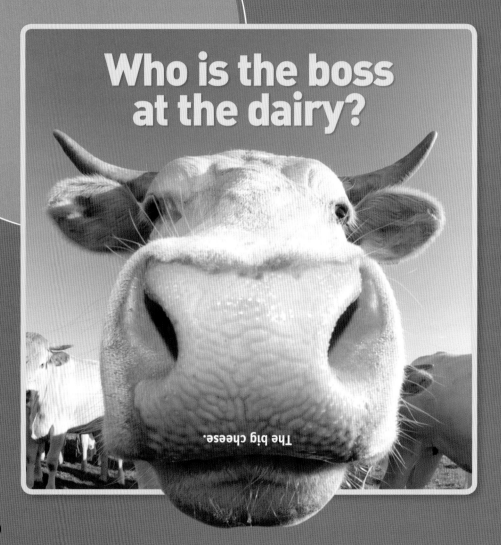

Who is the boss at the dairy?

The big cheese.

Q What did the
digital watch
say to the
grandfather
clock?

A "Look, Grandpa, no hands."

Q What did the blanket say to the bed?

A "Got you covered."

Q What do you say when you meet a two-headed monster?

A "Hello, hello."

Q **A man rode into town on Friday, stayed for 5 days, and then rode home on Friday.**
How is this possible?

A His horse was named Friday.

Q What do you call an elephant at the North Pole?

A Lost.

Q Who makes a living while driving **customers** away?

A A taxi driver.

Q What do cats like to eat for breakfast?

A Mice crispies.

92

What do you get
when you cross
a snowman
with a shark?

Frostbite.

93

95

What country

did candy come from?

Sweeten.

A bearded dragon's "beard" is a spike-filled throat pouch that it puffs out for protection.

KNOCK, KNOCK.

Who's there?
Walrus.
Walrus who?
Why do you walrus ask that silly question?

Q What did the duck say to the bunny?

A "You quack me up!"

Q

What do you call it when **crooks** go surfing?

A crime wave.

A

Q Why did the **baby cookie** cry?

A Because its mother was a wafer so long.

TONGUE TWISTER!

Say this fast three times:

Girl gargoyle, guy gargoyle.

Two snakes are talking.
SNAKE 1: "Are we venomous?"
SNAKE 2: "Yes, why?"
SNAKE 1: "I just bit my lip."

Q If the dictionary goes from **A to Z,** what goes from **Z to A?**

A A zebra.

KNOCK,
KNOCK.

Who's there?
Little old lady.
Little old lady who?
Hey, why are
you yodeling?

This African
leopard's spots,
called rosettes,
help it blend into
its surroundings.

101

What did the
window
say to the
door?

"What are you squeaking about?
I'm the one with the panes!"

This tropical rainbow toucan sleeps by folding its tail over its head and resting its long bill over its back.

104

JULIE: What's the difference between a chimp and a pizza?

JOHN: I don't know.

JULIE: Remind me not to send you to the grocery store!

Q **What kind of bird can write?**

A A penguin.

Q **How do you close an envelope underwater?**

A With a seal.

Q Why did the guy put a stove in his car?

A To make a hot rod.

Q What did the hat say to the scarf?

A You go around while I go on ahead.

Q What do you get when you cross a **fish** with an **elephant?**

A Swimming trunks.

Q How do you warm up a **room** after it's been **painted?**

A Give it a second coat.

CUSTOMER: "There's a dead beetle in my soup."

WAITER: "Yes, sir, they're not very good swimmers."

What happens when you tell an egg a **joke?**

It cracks up.

Tigers have been known to eat up to 60 pounds (27 kg) of meat in one night.

KNOCK, KNOCK.

Who's there?
Alaska.
Alaska who?
Alaska only one more time to open the door.

108

Q Have you ever seen a line drive?

A No, but I've seen a ballpark.

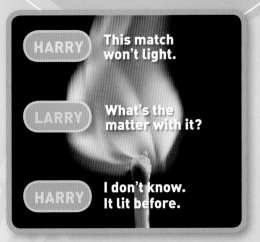

HARRY: This match won't light.

LARRY: What's the matter with it?

HARRY: I don't know. It lit before.

A pig is born with 28 baby teeth that later fall out.

KNOCK, KNOCK.

Who's there?
Dozen.
Dozen who?
Dozen anybody want to play with me?

110

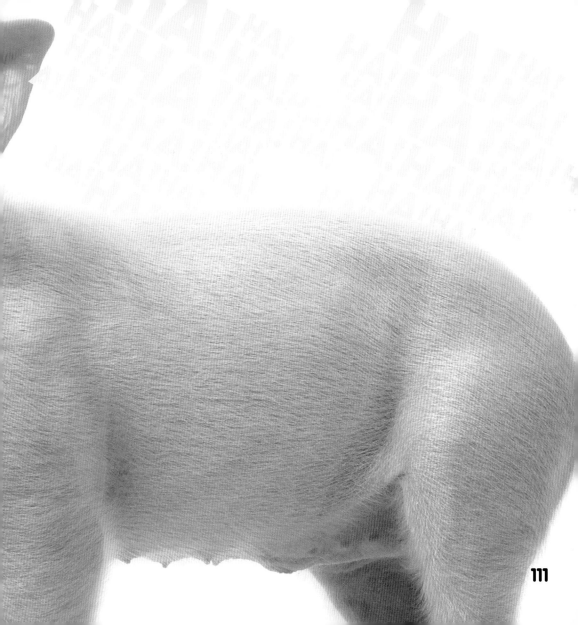

Q What do snowmen wear on their heads?

A Ice caps.

Q Where do snowflakes dance?

A At a snow ball.

112

Caribou are the only deer species in which both males and females have antlers.

KNOCK, KNOCK.

Who's there?
Luke.
Luke who?
Luke through the peephole and you'll see.

113

Red bulb,

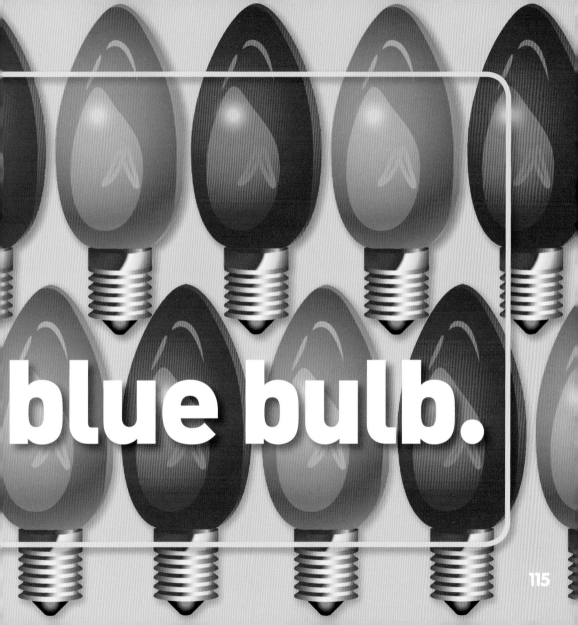

blue bulb.

Scientists think cats like this tabby kitten started living with humans about 9,000 years ago.

KNOCK, KNOCK.

Who's there?
Holly.
Holly who?
Holly days
are here again.

Q Why wouldn't they let the butterfly into the dance?

A Because it was a moth ball.

117

TONGUE TWISTER!

Say this fast three times:

At eight Edgar ate eight eggs.

Q Why did the cowboy put his bunk in the fireplace?

A So he could sleep like a log.

Q Why did the farmer's wife chase the chickens out of the yard?

A They were using fowl language.

Q What do you give an elephant that's going to be sick?

A Plenty of room.

118

Why did the **tomato** blush?

Because it saw the salad dressing.

119

120

Golden mantella frogs live on the African island of Madagascar and can be yellow, orange, or red.

A Hermann's tortoise can live for up to 30 years.

KNOCK, KNOCK.

Who's there?
Gorilla.
Gorilla who?
Gorilla me a steak.

Did you hear about the long-distance runner who took part in a 50-mile race? He was in the lead and had one more mile to go, but he was too tired to finish. So he turned around and ran back!

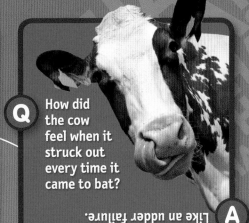

Q How did the cow feel when it struck out every time it came to bat?

A Like an udder failure.

Q What rock group has **four men** who **don't sing?**

A Mount Rushmore.

Q Why did the **gum** cross the road?

A Because it was stuck on the chicken's foot.

Q How do you keep a turkey in suspense?

A I'll tell you later!

TONGUE TWISTER!

Say this fast three times:

Six smart sharks swam swiftly.

Q What did the **bee** sit on?

A Its bee-hind.

Say this fast three times:

Double bubble gum bubbles double.

Why do hummingbirds hum?

Hmmmm.

Because they forgot the words.

Koalas spend as many as 18 hours a day napping or resting.

KNOCK, KNOCK.

Who's there?
Justin.
Justin who?
Justin the neighborhood.
Thought I'd stop by.

128

Q What happens when you annoy a clock?

A It gets ticked off!

TONGUE TWISTER!

Say this fast three times:

See me sneak in my squeaky, reeking sneakers.

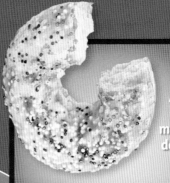

TONGUE TWISTER!

Say this fast three times:

Two twins twirled twelve tires.

Q What did the baseball glove say to the baseball?

A Catch you later.

130

Squirrel monkeys live in groups of up to 100 members.

KNOCK, KNOCK.
Who's there?
T-rex.
T-rex who?
There's a T-rex at your door and you want to know its name?

131

Most geckos have transparent eyelids that they keep clean with their tongues.

KNOCK, KNOCK.

Who's there?
Phillip.
Phillip who?
Phillip my bag with treats, please.

132

Say this fast three times:

If a black bug bleeds black blood, what color blood does a blue bug bleed?

Q Why couldn't the teddy bear eat his dessert?

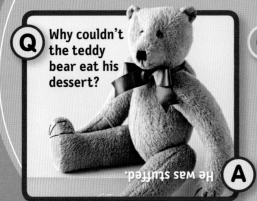

A He was stuffed.

Q What would you get if you crossed a judge with poison ivy?

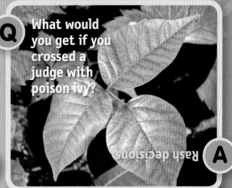

A Rash decisions.

Q What did the beaver say to the log?

A "It's been nice gnawing you."

Q What is the worst thing you're likely to find in a school **cafeteria?**

A The food.

TONGUE TWISTER!

Say this fast three times:

Sally saw Shelley singing swimming songs.

Q

What do you call a mom or dad you can **see** through?

Transparent.

A

136

Dogs sleep 12 hours a day on average.

137

I wish to wish the wish you wish to wish, but if you wish the wish the witch wishes, I won't wish the wish you wish to wish.

KNOCK, KNOCK.

Who's there?
D1.
D1 who?
D1 who knocked!

To evade predators, a puffer fish balloons up by filling its stomach with huge amounts of water.

Q Why do gorillas have big nostrils?

A Because they have big fingers.

Q Why are the rates at the Bird Paradise Hotel so much better than at other four-star hotels?

A Toucan stay for the price of one.

Q What kind of suit does a duck wear?

A A dux-edo.

Q Why did the **tonsils** get dressed up?

A Because the doctor was taking them out.

CUSTOMER:
Waitress, there's a fly in my soup!

WAITRESS:
Don't worry. We won't charge you extra for it.

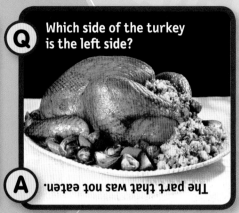

Q Which side of the turkey is the left side?

A The part that was not eaten.

Q

Why do soccer players do well in school?

Because they use their heads.

A

TONGUE TWISTER!

Say this fast three times:

Two totally tired toads tripped.

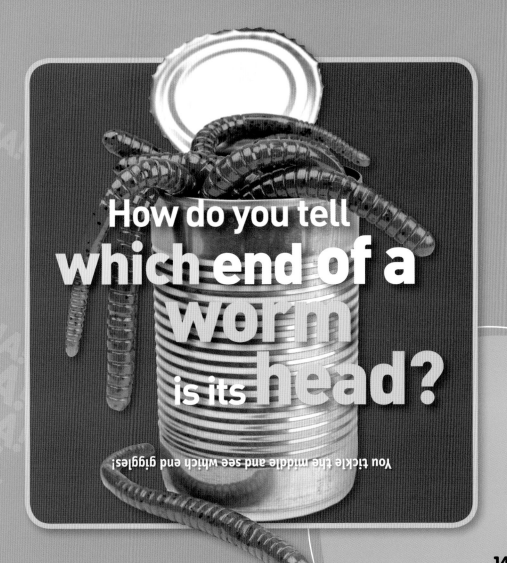

How do you tell which end of a worm is its head?

You tickle the middle and see which end giggles!

143

A group of mallard ducks in flight is called a sord.

144

145

While turtles live in almost any habitat, tortoises live on land.

What do you get when you cross a tortoise and a porcupine?

A porcupine's Latin name, *Erethizon dorsatum*, means "quill pig."

A slowpoke.

As many as 750 baboons, like this Hamadryas baboon, will sleep together for protection from predators.

KNOCK, KNOCK.

Who's there?
Cows go.
Cows go who?
No, silly. Cows go moo.

TONGUE TWISTER!

Say this fast three times:

Three free thoughtful seals.

Q

Why is it hard to carry on a conversation with a goat?

A They're always butting in.

149

Q Can you name the capital of all U.S. states in two seconds?

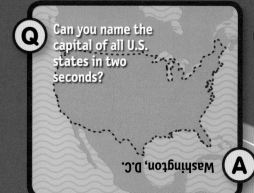

A Washington, D.C.

Q Why did the **football** coach go to the bank?

A To get his quarter back.

Q Why does the **ocean** roar?

A You'd roar too if you had crabs on your bottom.

Q Why couldn't the bicycle stand up?

A Because it was two tired.

HA!HA!HA!HA!HA!HA!HA!

What do you call a pig with three eyes?

A piiig.

Six slick sight

seers click.

153

Only the male impalas have long, ridged horns.

KNOCK, KNOCK.

Who's there?
Boo.
Boo who?
There, there. Please don't cry.

154

Q What did the smashed banana say when an elephant sat on it?

A Nothing. Bananas don't talk.

Q Why was the piano on the porch?

A Because it lost its keys.

Q What do you call a grizzly bear with no teeth?

A A gummy bear.

Q What do you do if a **teacher** rolls her eyes at you?

A Pick them up and roll them back to her.

Q What takes **dentists** on short trips?

A The tooth ferry.

Q What did one broom say to the other broom?

A "Have you heard the latest dirt?"

The Arabian stallion is one of the world's oldest breeds of riding horse.

KNOCK, KNOCK.

Who's there?
Amos.
Amos who?
A mosquito bit me.

157

The African penguin makes a donkeylike braying sound.

158

159

Why did the **spider** cross the road?

To get to the other Web site.

160

Q What do you call a rabbit that is owned by a beetle?

A A bug's bunny.

Q If a runner gets athlete's foot, what does an astronaut get?

A Missile toe.

Q Why did the lion spit out the clown?

A Because he tasted funny.

Q What do you do when your **poodle** won't stop **sneezing?**

A Call a dog-tor.

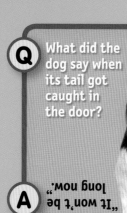

Q What did the dog say when its tail got caught in the door?

A "It won't be long now."

Q What do you get when you cross a caterpillar with a parrot?

A A walkie-talkie.

HA!HA!HA!
HA!HA!HA!
HA!HA!HA!
HA!HA!HA!
HA!HA!HA!
HA!HA!HA!

KNOCK, KNOCK.

Who's there?
Roach.
Roach who?
Roach you a good letter.
Did you get it?

This agamid lizard lives in Indonesia.

163

Is it hard to spot

a leopard?

No, they come that way!

Red foxes prey on small game, such as rabbits, rodents, and birds.

166

Say this fast three times:

The ocean sure soaked Sherman.

What did the pelican say when it finished shopping?

Q

A "Put it on my bill."

Donkeys are the smallest members of the horse family.

169

Q What starts with an e, ends in an e, but only has one **letter?**

A An envelope.

Q What sports are trains good at?

A Track events.

Q Why is basketball such a messy sport?

A Because the players dribble all over the court.

Q What has more lives than a cat?
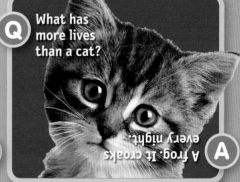
A A frog. It croaks every night.

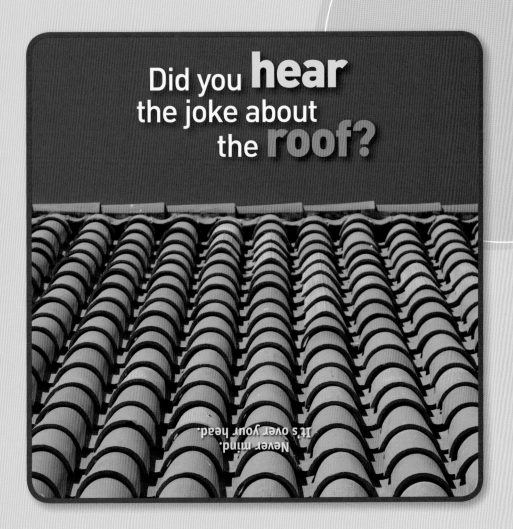

Did you **hear** the joke about the **roof?**

Never mind. It's over your head.

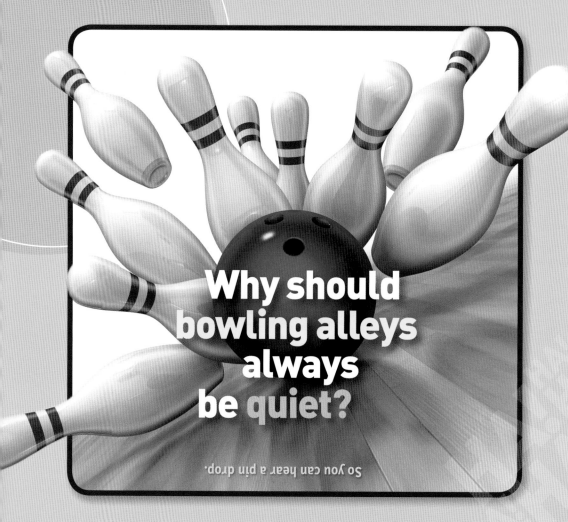

Why should bowling alleys always be quiet?

So you can hear a pin drop.

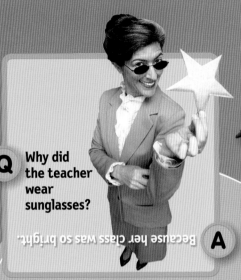

Q Why did the teacher wear sunglasses?

A Because her class was so bright.

Q What do you call a computer superhero?

A A screen saver.

Q Have you heard about the new **restaurant** on the **moon?**

A It's got great food but no atmosphere.

TONGUE TWISTER!

Say this fast three times:

Katie's kittens caught Kyle's kite.

Q What is a volcano?

A A mountain with hiccups.

Q What has 50 **heads** and 50 **tails?**

A A roll of pennies.

TONGUE TWISTER!

Say this fast three times:

Three **free** throws.

Q What do you give a dog with a fever?

A Mustard. It's the best thing for a hot dog!

KNOCK,

KNOCK.

Who's there?
Zombies.
Zombies who?
Zombies make
honey and zombies
don't.

Sound waves travel through a hippopotamus's jaws, allowing it to hear underwater.

175

A gazillion gig gushed giving gophers

antic grapes
gradually
gooey guts.

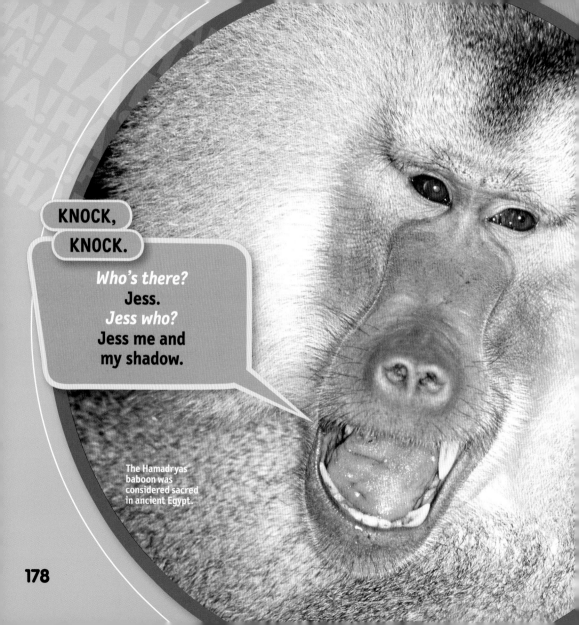

KNOCK, KNOCK.

Who's there?
Jess.
Jess who?
Jess me and my shadow.

The Hamadryas baboon was considered sacred in ancient Egypt.

Q

Why do magicians
do so well in school?

They're good at trick questions.

A

TONGUE
TWISTER!

Say this fast three times:

**A big black bug
bit a big black bear.**

Q How do you catch a squirrel?

A Climb a tree and act like a nut!

Say this fast three times:

Felix finds fresh french fries finer.

Q Why did the **computer** go to the orthodontist?

A To improve its byte.

A parrot snake's fangs are located in the back of its mouth.

181

Macaws can live to be 65 years old.

183

Say this fast three times:

Crisp crusts crackle and crunch.

Q **Why couldn't anyone find the deck of cards?**

A They got lost in the shuffle.

Q Why didn't the duck doctor have any patients?

A Everyone knew he was a quack.

Q What did the bee say to the flower?

A "Hey, bud. When do you open?"

Q **Why did the traffic light turn red?**

A Wouldn't you if you had to change in the middle of the street?

Q Why don't mummies go on vacation?

A They're afraid they might unwind.

Q What did one potato chip say to the other?

A "Shall we go for a dip?"

Young Amazon river dolphins are dark gray, but adults are solid pink or have pink blotches.

HA! HA! HA! HA! HA! HA! HA! HA! HA!

What do you call

a fake noodle?

An impasta.

Polar bears have been spotted on sea ice hundreds of miles from shore.

KNOCK, KNOCK.

Who's there?
Eiffel.
Eiffel who?
Eiffel down the steps.

190

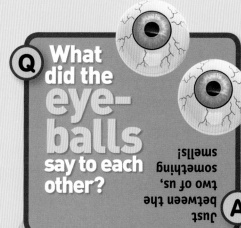

Q What did the **eye-balls** say to each other?

A Just between the two of us, something smells!

A snail is robbed by four turtles. When he goes to the police, the officer asks, "Can you describe the turtles?"

The snail replies, "Not well. It all happened so fast."

Q What kind of **animal** would you **never** play **video games** with?

A A cheetah.

Q Where do **crayons** go on **vacation?**

A To a wax museum.

Q

What do you get
if you cross a

dinosaur

with a **pig?**

A Jurassic-pork.

Q Why was the
man fired from
the orange juice
factory?

A Because he couldn't
concentrate.

FATHER How are your grades, son?

SON Underwater, Dad.

FATHER Underwater? What
do you mean?

SON They're below C level.

Q Where was
the Declaration
of Independence
signed?

At the bottom. **A**

192

The ornate horned frog is sometimes called a Pac-Man frog—after the classic video game—because of its large mouth.

KNOCK, KNOCK.

Who's there?
Shirley.
Shirley who?
Shirley you know my name by now.

193

194

Burmese pythons are among the largest snakes on Earth, sometimes growing as wide as a telephone pole.

A mouse opossum's tail can be as long as the rest of its body.

KNOCK, KNOCK.

Who's there?
Meyer.
Meyer who?
Meyer nosy!

196

Say this fast three times:

Roscoe rescued Rosie from roaring rapids.

Q Why did the Pilgrims' pants keep falling down?

A Because their belt buckles were on their hats.

Q

What do
you call a
pig
that does karate?

A pork chop.

A

Q

Why are
giraffes
so slow to
apologize?

A

Because it takes
them a long time
to swallow
their pride.

Q What does
**lightning put on
during
rainy weather?**

Thunderwear.

A

What do you call a rooster who wakes you up at the same time every morning?

An alarm cluck.

Adult male chickens are called roosters; young male chickens are called cockerels.

199

HA!HA!HA!HA!HA!HA!HA!HA!HA!HA!HA!HA!HA!HA!HA!

Orangutans find water to drink inside tree hollows, on wet leaves, or even on their own fur after a rain.

201

JOKEFINDER

JOKEFINDER

Tongue twisters

ILLUSTRATIONCREDITS

92 (left), Andy Rouse/NHPA/PS; 92 (background), Aflo/ naturepl.com; 93 (left), angelo gilardelli/SS; 93 (right), Rich Carey/SS; 94, Chris Fourie/SS; 96-101, Michal Vitek/ SS; 98, Ashley Whitworth/SS; 99, Richard Peterson/SS; 100 (top), Tony Savino/CB; 100 (bottom, left), Stephen Dalton/NHPA/PS; 100 (bottom, right), Stephen Dalton/ NHPA/PS; 101, HPH Image Library/SS; 103 (right), C./SS; 103 (left), sabri deniz kizil/SS; 104, mountainpix/SS; 105 (bottom), Anthony Berenyi/SS; 105 (top), Eric Isselée/SS; 106 (left), Andy Crawford/GI; 106 (right), William Joseph Boch Photography/StockFood; 106 (right inset), Joel Sartore/NGS; 107, Peter Zijlstra/SS; 108, Dariush M./ SS; 109 (top), Stephen Mcsween/SS; 109 (bottom), Kasza/ SS; 110-109, Corbis/SK; 112 (bottom), Myoko Komine/ amana images/GI; 112 (top), Gorilla/SS; 113, Tom & Pat Leeson; 114-115, CRWPitman/SS; 114-115, CRWPitman/ SS; 116, Foonia/SS; 117, James Laurie/SS; 118 (top, left), Seregam/SS; 118 (top, right), patti jean_images & designs by patti jean guerrero/SS; 118 (bottom, left), Radu Razvan/SS; 118 (bottom, right), Ryan Mcvay/GI; 119, topseller/SS; 120-121, Joel Sartore; 122, Quayside/SS; 123 (left), Digital Vision/SS; 123 (right), Kurt De Bruyn/SS; 124 (bottom, right), Dima Fadev/SS; 124 (bottom, left), Jeff Hunter/GI; 124 (top), Digital Vision/GI; 125, Stephen Coburn/SS; 126-127, Luis Francisco Cordero/SS; 128, Darrell Gulin/GI; 129 (bottom), Photodisc Green/GI; 129 (top), AnatolyM/SS; 130 (bottom, right), Svetlana Larina/ SS; 130 (top, right), oksana2010/SS; 130 (left), Bill Losh/ GI; 131, Helen E. Grose/SS; 132-133, irin-k/SS; 134 (top), Bambuh/SS; 135 (top, right), Chris Hill/SS; 135 (bottom), Alan & Sandy Carey/OSF/Animals Animals; 135 (top, left), Larry Lilac/Alamy; 136 (top), Rubberball Productions/GI; 137, B&T Media Group Inc./SS; 139 (center), Poznyakov/ SS; 139 (front, center), Dan Lee/SS; 140, Steven Hunt/ The Image Bank/GI; 141 (top, left), Michael Nichols/NGS; 141 (top, right), Gerry Ellis/GI; 141 (bottom, left), Terry Alexander/SS; 142 (left), Comstock/JI; 142 (top, right), Spencer Jones/GI; 142 (bottom, right), Eric Isselée/SS; 143, James Steidl/SS; 144-145, Jane Burton/naturepl. com; 146, BananaStock/JI; 147, Eric Isselée/SS; 148, Brian Kenney; 149 (top), Royalty-Free/CB; 149 (bottom),

Pavelk/SS; 150 (bottom), Redlink/CB; 151, Yakovleva Zinaida Vasilevna/SS; 152-153, Thomas Hoeffgen/GI; Bruce Coleman, Inc./PS; 155 (top), foodanddrinkphotos. com; 155 (bottom), Kelly Redinger/Design Pics/CB; 156 (left), Suzi Eszterhas/MP; 156, hansenn/SS; 157, Fotopic/ Index Stock Imagery, Inc./photolibrary.com; 158-159, Luciano Candisani/MP; 160 (background), Nicemonkey/ SS; 160 (center), Jacob Hamblin/SS; 161 (top, left), Imageman/SS; 161 (top, right), NASA; 161 (bottom), Paul Souders/GI; 162 (top), Eric Isselée/SS; 162 (bottom), Eric Isselée/SS; 163, Ch'ien Lee/MP; 164, Tatiana Morozova/ SS; 166, David Courtenay/GI; 167, Tramont_ana/SS; 168-171, Armin Rose/SS; 170 (top), Michael G Smith/ SS; 170 (bottom, right), Jiri Hera/SS; 170 (bottom, left), Alexander Raths/SS; 171, Lucertolone/SS; 172, Solvod/ SS; 173 (left), Royalty-Free/CB; 173 (top, right), AISPIX/ SS; 173 (bottom, right), bezmaski/SS; 174 (top), James L. Amos/NGS; 174 (bottom), BananaStock/JI; 175, Gert Johannes Jacobus Vrey/SS; 176-177, Adisa/SS; 178, G. C. Kelley/Photo Researchers, Inc.; 179 (top), G. K. & Vikki Hart/GI; 179 (bottom), nialat/SS; 180 (left), KV4000/SS; 180 (top), Burke/Triolo/Brand X Pictures/PictureQuest; 181, Theo Allofs/zefa/CB; 182-183, Vivid Pixels/SS; 184, Irina Rogova/SS; 185 (top), Royalty-Free/CB; 185 (bottom), manfredxy/SS; 186 (top), pzAxe/SS; 186 (bottom), AGphotographer/SS; 187, Kevin Schafer/MP; 188, Sailorr/ SS; 190, ZSSD/MP; 191 (top, left), Comstock/JI; 191 (top, right), Radius/SK; 191 (bottom, right), Image Source/GI; 192 (left), Specta/SS; 192 (right), Inga Nielsen/SS; 193, Zig Leszczynski/Animals Animals; 194-195, Jane Burton/ naturepl.com; 196, Haroldo Palo Jr./NHPA/PS; 197 (top), Skip Brown/NGS; 197 (bottom), Photodisc Green/GI; 198 (top, left), akva/SS; 198 (top, right), Anky/SS; 198 (bottom), Jhaz Photography/SS; 199, Ursula/SS; 200, DLILLC/ CB; 202, Winfried Wisniewski/zefa/CB.

Published by the National Geographic Society
John M. Fahey, Jr., *Chairman of the Board and Chief Executive Officer*
Timothy T. Kelly, *President*
Declan Moore, *Executive Vice President; President, Publishing*
Melina Gerosa Bellows, *Executive Vice President; Chief Creative Officer, Books, Kids, and Family*

Prepared by the Book Division
Nancy Laties Feresten, *Senior Vice President, Editor in Chief, Children's Books*
Jonathan Halling, *Design Director, Books and Children's Publishing*
Jay Sumner, *Director of Photography, Children's Publishing*
Jennifer Emmett, *Editorial Director, Children's Books*
Carl Mehler, *Director of Maps*
R. Gary Colbert, *Production Director*
Jennifer A. Thornton, *Managing Editor*

Based on the "Just Joking" department in
National Geographic Kids **magazine**
Kelley Miller, *Senior Photo Editor*
Julide Dengel, *Designer*
Margaret Krauss, *Researcher*

Staff for This Book
Robin Terry, *Project Editor*
Eva Absher, *Managing Art Director*
Kelley Miller, *Illustrations Editor*
David M. Seager, *Art Director/Designer*
Grace Hill, *Associate Managing Editor*
Joan Gossett, *Production Editor*
Lewis R. Bassford, *Production Manager*
Susan Borke, *Legal and Business Affairs*
Kate Olesin, *Assistant Editor*
Kathryn Robbins, *Design Production Assistant*
Hillary Moloney, *Illustrations Assistant*
Jean Mendoza, Catherine Monson, *Editorial Interns*

Manufacturing and Quality Management
Christopher A. Liedel, *Chief Financial Officer*
Phillip L. Schlosser, *Senior Vice President*
Chris Brown, *Technical Director*
Nicole Elliott, *Manager*
Rachel Faulise, *Manager*
Robert L. Barr, *Manager*

The National Geographic Society is one of the world's largest nonprofit scientific and educational organizations. Founded in 1888 to "increase and diffuse geographic knowledge," the Society works to inspire people to care about the planet. National Geographic reflects the world through its magazines, television programs, films, music and radio, books, DVDs, maps, exhibitions, live events, school publishing programs, interactive media and merchandise. *National Geographic* magazine, the Society's official journal, published in English and 33 local-language editions, is read by more than 38 million people each month. The National Geographic Channel reaches 320 million households in 34 languages in 166 countries. National Geographic Digital Media receives more than 15 million visitors a month. National Geographic has funded more than 9,400 scientific research, conservation and exploration projects and supports an education program promoting geography literacy. For more information, visit nationalgeographic.com.

For more information, please call 1-800-NGS LINE (647-5463)
or write to the following address:
National Geographic Society
1145 17th Street N.W.
Washington, D.C. 20036-4688 U.S.A.

Visit us online at nationalgeographic.com/books

For librarians and teachers: ngchildrensbooks.org

More for kids from National Geographic: kids.nationalgeographic.com

For information about special discounts for bulk purchases, please contact National Geographic Books Special Sales: ngspecsales@ngs.org

For rights or permissions inquiries, please contact National Geographic Books Subsidiary Rights: ngbookrights@ngs.org

Library of Congress Cataloging-in-Publication Data

Just joking: 300 hilarious jokes, tricky tongue twisters, and ridiculous riddles / by National Geographic kids.
    p. cm.
    ISBN 978-1-4263-0930-4 (pbk. : alk. paper)—ISBN 978-1-4263-0944-1 (library binding : alk. paper)
    1. Wit and humor, Juvenile. I. National Geographic Society (U.S.)
    PN6166.J87 2012
    818'.602—dc22

                        2011034649

Printed in China
14/PPS/5

NATIONAL GEOGRAPHIC
KIDS

Just Joking 2

300 hilarious jokes about everything, including tongue twisters, riddles, and more!

NATIONAL
GEOGRAPHIC

WASHINGTON, D.C.

Snow leopards are rare cats that live in the mountains of Central Asia.

4

5

KNOCK, KNOCK.

Who's there?
Honeybee.
Honeybee who?
Honey, be a dear and get me a soda.

6

The orangutan is the world's largest tree-dwelling animal.

TONGUE TWISTER!

Say this fast three times:

Fred threw thirty-three free throws.

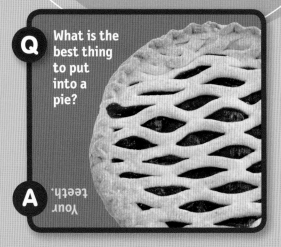

Q What is the best thing to put into a pie?

A Your teeth.

BOY Are caterpillars good to eat?

FATHER No. Why do you ask?

BOY You had one in your salad, but it's gone now.

Q What colors would you paint the sun and the wind?

A The sun rose and the wind blue.

Q What do farmers give their sweethearts for Valentine's Day?

A A hog and a kiss.

Q Why is slippery pavement like music?

A If you don't C sharp, you'll B flat!

IT'S LOVE

MY BABY

Madagascar is home to about 150 chameleon species, including this Boettger's chameleon.

9

10

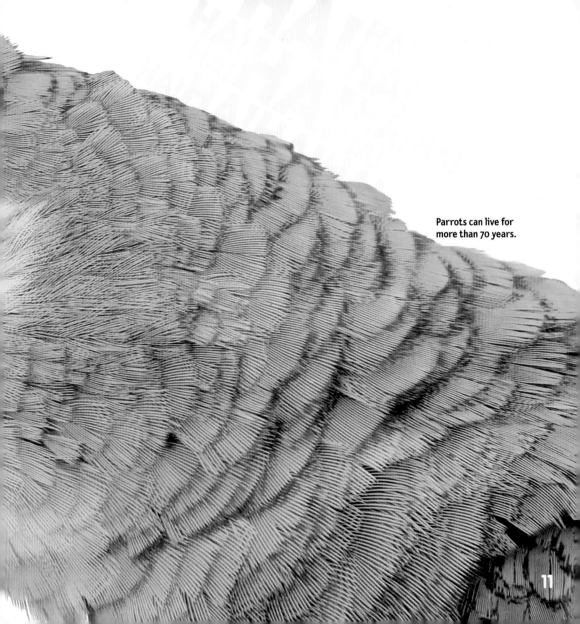

Parrots can live for more than 70 years.

11

Q What did one volcano say to the other volcano?

A I lava you.

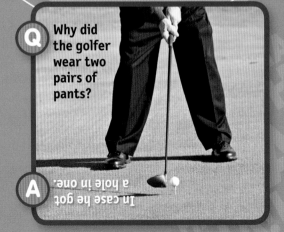

Q Why did the golfer wear two pairs of pants?

A In case he got a hole in one.

12

Parrot snakes are found in southern Mexico and South America.

KNOCK, KNOCK.

Who's there?
Says.
Says who?
Says me, that's who!

13

Flamingos use mouthfuls of mud to build their nests.

Why are **flamingos** always happy?

Because they are never blue.

TONGUE TWISTER!

Say this fast three times:

Kent sent Trent to the tent.

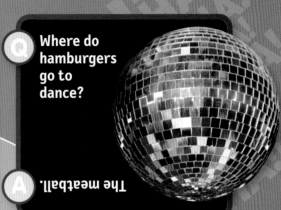

Q Where do hamburgers go to dance?

A The meatball.

Q Why did the kid put ice in his aunt's bed?

A He wanted to make auntifreeze.

Q What **room** has no floor, windows, or doors?

A A mushroom!

15

Bob brought back from the

blue balloons big bazaar.

A hippopotamus can hold its breath underwater for up to five minutes.

KNOCK, KNOCK.

Who's there?
Mary Lee.
Mary Lee who?
Mary Lee down the stream.

18

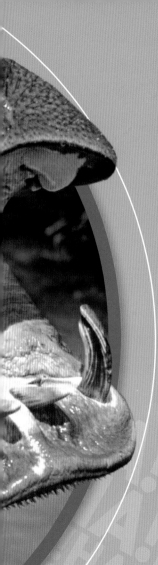

 Q From what word can you take away *the whole* and still have *some left?*

A Wholesome.

TONGUE TWISTER!

Say this fast three times:

Old oily Olly oils old oily autos.

19

TONGUE TWISTER!

Say this fast three times:

Skunks sat on a stump and the stump stunk.

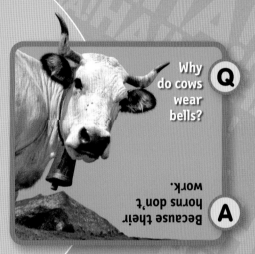

Q Why do cows wear bells?

A Because their horns don't work.

Q What can a whole orange do that a half an orange can't do?

A Look round.

Q What goes **up** but never comes down?

A Your age.

KNOCK, KNOCK.

Who's there?
Xavier.
Xavier who?
Xavier breath
and open
that door.

This bird, called a bee-eater, can capture prey while flying.

21

Box turtles burrow up to two feet into the ground for hibernation.

23

Hawaiian monk seals weigh up to 600 pounds (272 kg)—as much as a small horse!

KNOCK, KNOCK.

Who's there?
Sam.
Sam who?
Sam person who knocked before!

24

Q What do dentists call their x-rays?

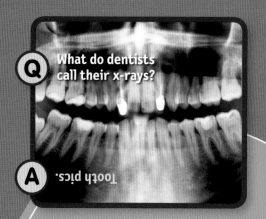

A Tooth pics.

Q What did **Robin Hood** have when the arrow fired at him missed?

A An-arrow escape!

Q What happened to the cat who swallowed a ball of wool?

Q She had mittens.

Q What happened after the girl drank eight sodas?

A She burped seven up.

DOCTOR:
Nurse, did you take the patient's temperature?

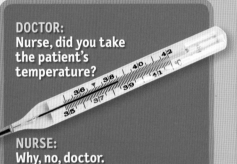

NURSE:
Why, no, doctor. Is it missing?

Q

Why did the kid **eat** his homework?

Because his teacher said it was a piece of cake.

A

Q

What did the **grape** do when it got stepped on?

It let out a little wine.

A

What is a witch's favorite subject in school?

Q

Spelling.

A

Chimpanzee calls can be heard a mile away.

KNOCK, KNOCK.

Who's there?
Cousin.
Cousin who?
Cousin stead of opening the door, you're making me stand here.

27

It takes up to 26 hours for a hen to lay just one egg.

Why do
hens lay
eggs?

Because they break if they drop them.

29

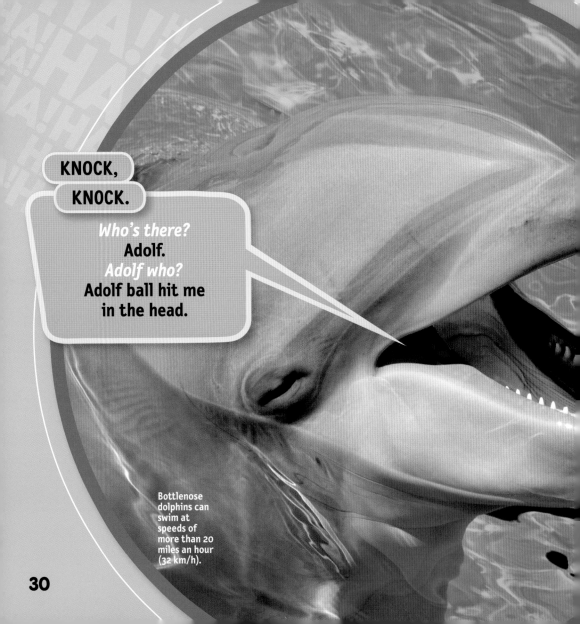

KNOCK,
KNOCK.

Who's there?
Adolf.
Adolf who?
Adolf ball hit me
in the head.

Bottlenose
dolphins can
swim at
speeds of
more than 20
miles an hour
(32 km/h).

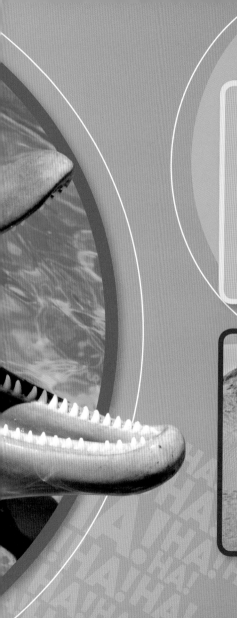

What is
the richest
kind of
air?

Millionaire.

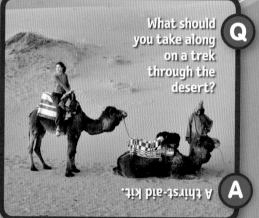

What should
you take along
on a trek
through the
desert?

A thirst-aid kit.

31

Q Why did the farmer's wife chase the chickens out of the yard?

A They were using fowl language.

Q What kind of car does a rich cow drive?

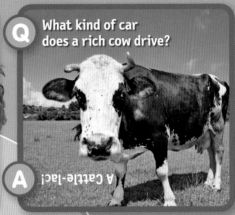

A A Cattle-lac!

SUE: Look—there's a baby snake.

LOU: How do you know it's a baby?

SUE: You can tell by its rattle!

Q What did the **hat** say to the **hat rack?**

A "You stay here. I'll go on ahead."

Black bears "clack" their teeth when frightened.

33

34

Zebras make
braying, barking, and
snorting sounds.

35

How much does it cost a
pirate
to get his ears pierced?

A buck an ear.

Q Why was the farmer famous?

A He was outstanding in his field.

Say this fast three times:

Shelter for six sick scenic sightseers.

Q

How did the **tree** feel after the beaver left?

A "Gnawed" so good.

Q Where do snowmen put their Web pages?

A On the Winter-net.

37

Q What sports are trains good at?

A Track events.

Q What did the **wind** say to the **screen door?**

A "Just passing through."

Gray wolves consume up to 20 pounds (9 kg) of meat in one meal.

HA!HA! HA! HA! HA! HA! HA! HA! HA! HA! HA!HA! HA!HA! HA!HA!

38

39

Say this fast three times:

Can canned cla

40

Clams can live in fresh water or salt water, buried up to two feet (0.6 m) deep in the sandy bottom.

ms can clams?

Merino sheep originated in Spain and are known for producing fine wool.

Where did the sheep get its hair cut?

At the baa-baa shop.

Q What is the elephant's favorite vegetable?

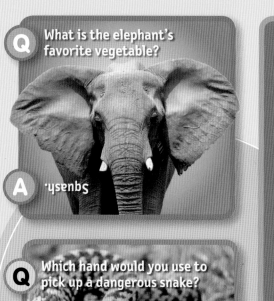

A Squash.

Q Which hand would you use to pick up a dangerous snake?

A Someone else's.

A police officer saw a woman in her car with a penguin. The officer said, "It's against the law to have that penguin in your car! Take it to the zoo."

The next day the police officer saw the same woman in her car with the same penguin. He said, "I told you to take that penguin to the zoo!"

The woman replied, "I did. He liked it so much, today we're going to the beach!"

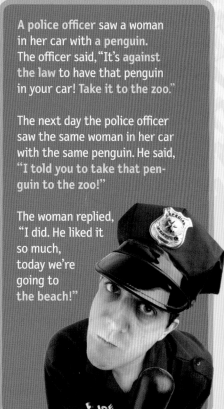

43

Caimans are related to alligators.

Why did the pony have a sore throat? **Q**

He was a little horse. **A**

Q

Why do elephants do well in school?

Because they have a lot of gray matter.

A

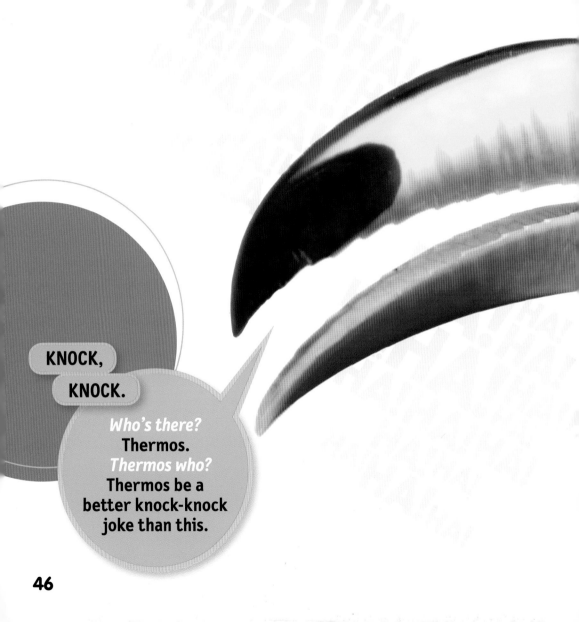

KNOCK,

KNOCK.

Who's there?
Thermos.
Thermos who?
Thermos be a
better knock-knock
joke than this.

46

A toucan does not
have a large bill when
it hatches; it takes a
few months for its bill
to become full size.

47

Q What part of the fish weighs the most?

A The scales.

Q What would you have if Batman and Robin were run over by stampeding cattle?

A Flatman and Ribbon.

Q Why is the letter *G* scary?

A It turns a host into a ghost.

Q What did the one lightning bolt say to the other lightning bolt?

A You're shocking!

48

Grasshoppers smell with organs located on their antennae.

What did the
grasshopper
say when it hit the
windshield?

"If I had the guts, I'd do it again."

Atlantic puffins breed in the North Atlantic, building nests atop rocky seaside cliffs.

50

Q What athlete can jump higher than a building?

A Any athlete—buildings can't jump!

Q What washes up on very small beaches?

A Micro-waves.

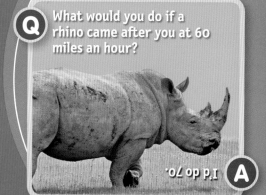

Q What would you do if a rhino came after you at 60 miles an hour?

A I'd do 70.

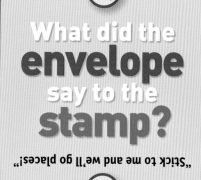

Q What did the **envelope** say to the **stamp?**

A "Stick to me and we'll go places!"

51

There are more than 45 recognized rabbit breeds in the United States alone.

52

What do you call a **a rabbit** who is really **cool?**

A hip hopper.

KNOCK,
KNOCK.

Who's there?
Island.
Island who?
Island on your roof with
my parachute.

54

Q What do you call a goat's beard?

A A goatee.

The buffy fish owl sometimes uses another bird's empty nest for itself.

TONGUE TWISTER!

Say this fast three times:

Walter wants winter weather.

Q Do **zombies** eat popcorn with their fingers?

A No—they eat the fingers separately.

Say this fast three times:

Dick kicks sticky **bricks.**

Q What color is a **burp?**

A Burple.

Q Why do dogs run in circles?

A Because it's hard to run in squares.

56

SOCCER PLAYER: Check it out—another straight-A report card.

TENNIS PLAYER: How do you do so well in school?

SOCCER PLAYER: I'm always using my head.

58

Ducks waddle because their feet are positioned close to their rear ends.

59

In a cold climate, a raccoon often doubles its body weight to prepare to sleep through the winter.

60

VOICE ON TELEPHONE: I'm afraid Karen won't be at school today.
PRINCIPAL: Who's calling?
VOICE: It's my mom.

Oops!

TONGUE TWISTER!

Say this fast three times:

Three free-thinking frogs think friendly thoughts.

Q What kind of driver **never** gets a **ticket?**

A screwdriver.

A

Q What kind of dinosaur is never late?

A "pronto-saurus."

A

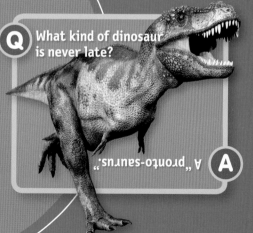

61

Q Why did the **penny,** but not the quarter, jump off the cliff?

A The quarter had more cents.

TONGUE TWISTER!

Say this fast three times:

Bobby Blue blew big blue bubbles.

Orcas are also called killer whales.

KNOCK, KNOCK.

Who's there?
Dots.
Dots who?
Dot's for me to know and you to find out.

63

What do you get when you cross a **snake** and a **Lego set?**

A boa constructor.

64

There are about 2,700 species of snakes, but only about 375 species, including this diamondback, are venomous.

65

Pelicans, such as this great white pelican, use their elastic pouches to catch fish.

66

Say this fast three times:

A shapeless **sash** sags slowly.

Q Why did the cheetah refuse to bathe in dishwashing detergent?

A He didn't want to come out spotless.

67

Q How is a **baseball team** similar to a **muffin?**

A They both depend on the batter.

Q Why did the scientist install a knocker on his door?

A To win the no-bell prize.

Q What do dogs do after they're through with obedience school?

A They get their masters.

Q What did the carpet say to the floor?

A "Don't worry. I'm on top of everything."

TONGUE TWISTER!

Say this fast three times:

Fussy Freddie flings food furiously.

Bats are
the only flying
mammals.

71

Harp seal mothers can identify their young by scent alone.

KNOCK,

KNOCK.

Who's there?
Albie.
Albie who?
Albie out here if you need me.

A duck walks into the drug-store to buy some lip balm. The cashier asks the duck, "Cash or charge?" The duck says, "Just put it on my bill."

Q

Why did the man run around his **bed**?

A To catch up on his sleep.

PATIENT:
What is the best way to prevent diseases caused by biting insects?

DOCTOR:
Don't bite any!

73

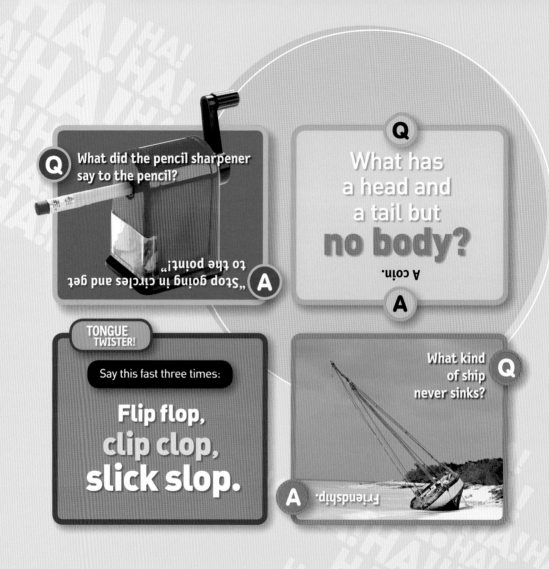

Q What did the pencil sharpener say to the pencil?

A "Stop going in circles and get to the point!"

Q What has a head and a tail but **no body?**

A A coin.

TONGUE TWISTER!

Say this fast three times:

Flip flop, clip clop, slick slop.

Q What kind of ship never sinks?

A Friendship.

Two thieves robbing an apartment hear the owner coming home.

"Quick, jump out the window," says the first robber.

"Are you crazy? We're on the 13th floor!" says the second robber.

The first one replies, "This is no time to be superstitious!"

Swan swam over the sea. Swim, swan, swim.

Swans mate for life.

Swan swam back again.
Well swum, swan!

A serval's hearing is so sensitive it can hear prey moving underground.

KNOCK, KNOCK.

Who's there?
Adore.
Adore who?
Adore stands between us. Open up!

78

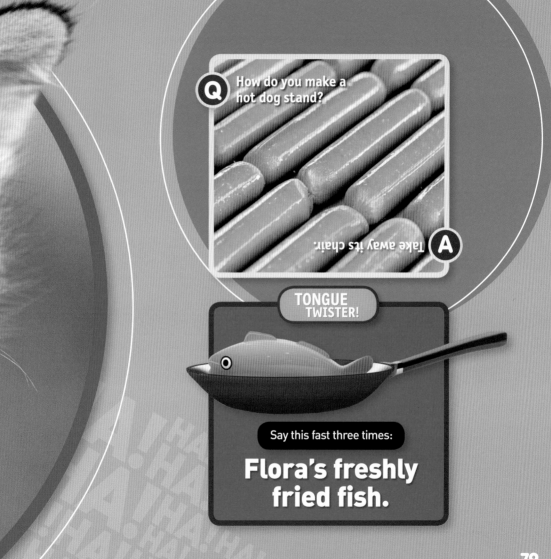

Q How do you make a hot dog stand?

A Take away its chair.

TONGUE TWISTER!

Say this fast three times:

Flora's freshly fried fish.

Q Why do bees have sticky hair?

A Because they have honeycombs.

Say this fast three times:

Mix, miss, mix!

Say this fast three times:

An ape hates grape cakes.

Q What is the **hottest** letter in the alphabet?

A B, because it makes oil ... Boil!

80

Donkeys are also called burros.

KNOCK, KNOCK.

Who's there?
Stopwatch.
Stopwatch who?
Stopwatch you're doing and open this door.

81

Cats can make
more than 100
vocal sounds.

83

Chameleons can move one eye at a time.

KNOCK, KNOCK.

Who's there?
Voodoo.
Voodoo who?
Voodoo you think
you are?

84

Q

What did one **flea** say to the other as they left the restaurant?

A "Shall we walk or take a dog?"

Q What do you say when a balloon pops?

A "May you rest in pieces."

Q What books did the owl like?

A Hoot-dunits!

Q

What has four **wheels** and flies?

A A garbage truck.

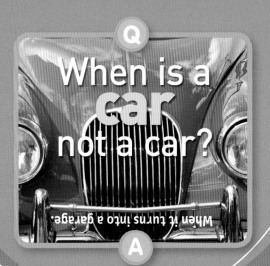

Q

When is a
car
not a car?

A

When it turns into a garage.

Q Why did the whale cross the road?

A To get to the other tide.

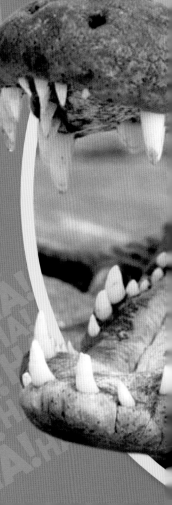

HA!HA!
HA!HA!
HA!HA!
HA!HA!

86

The Mugger crocodile can grow up to 16 feet (4.9 m) long—about the length of an SUV!

KNOCK,

KNOCK.

Who's there?
Theodore.
Theodore who?
Theodore wasn't open,
so I knocked.

87

Male peacocks use their colorful feathers to attract mates.

Where does a peacock go when it loses its tail?

A retail store.

89

A man rushes into the doctor's office and shouts, "Doctor! I think I'm shrinking!" The doctor calmly responds, "Now, settle down. You'll just have to be a little patient."

Q

Why was the archaeologist upset?

A

His job was in ruins.

Q Why did the gum cross the road?

A Because it was stuck to the chicken's foot.

Q Why are elephants wrinkled?

A Have you ever tried to iron one?

TONGUE TWISTER!

Say this fast three times:

Bob's big black bath brush broke.

91

Q

There are two farms next to each other. One is in Canada and one is in the United States. A rooster runs from the farm in Canada to the farm in the U.S. and lays an egg. So which country does the egg actually belong to?

A

Neither. Roosters don't lay eggs.

Q

How do **mermaids** keep in contact with each other?

A

They use their shell phones.

Q

How do you get rid of a boomerang?

A

Throw it down a one-way street.

92

An upset man calls the fire department to report a fire in his neighborhood.
The dispatcher asks him, "How do we get there?"
The man replies, "Don't you still have those big red trucks?"

93

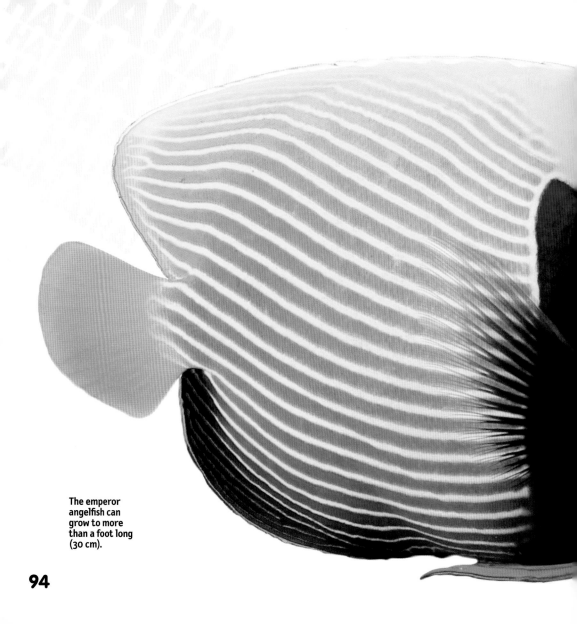

The emperor
angelfish can
grow to more
than a foot long
(30 cm).

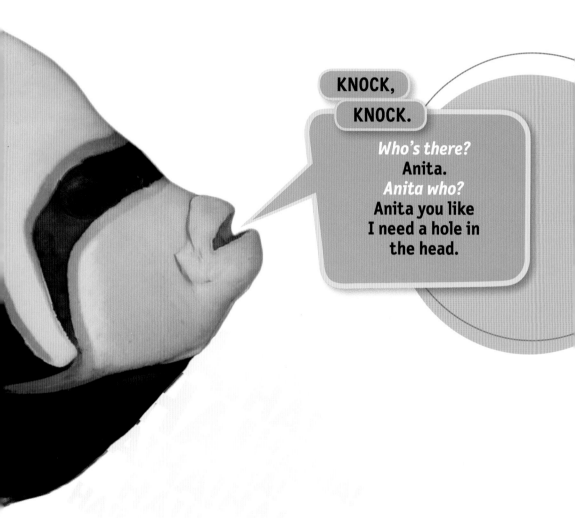

95

Fred fed Ted bread.

Ted fed
Fred bread.

97

KNOCK, KNOCK.

Who's there?
Ammonia.
Ammonia who?
Ammonia little kid.

The frilled lizard opens the hood around its neck to scare away predators.

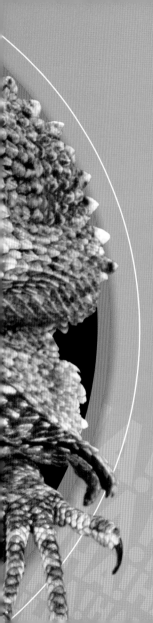

What jam can't be eaten on toast? Q

A A traffic jam.

Q

What weighs
5,000 lb.
and wears
glass slippers?

Cinderelephant.

A

99

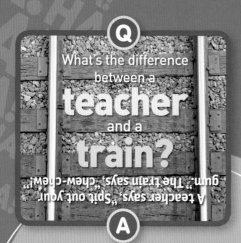

Q

What's the difference between a **teacher** and a **train?**

A

A teacher says, "Spit out your gum." The train says, "chew-chew!"

TONGUE TWISTER!

Say this fast three times:

Tiny turtles trotted to the track.

Q

What kind of birds stick together?

A Vel-crows.

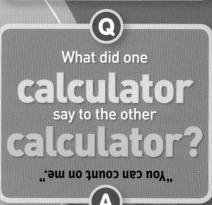

Q

What did one **calculator** say to the other **calculator?**

A "You can count on me."

Ostriches are the world's largest birds.

KNOCK, KNOCK.

Who's there?
Isaiah.
Isaiah who?
Isaiah nothing until you open this door.

101

Which
letters
are not

OPQUSTUVWXYZ
MLKJGIHFEDCBA
OPQUSTUVWXYZ
MLKJGIHFEDCBA
OPQUSTUVWXYZ
MLKJGIHFEDCBA
OPQUSTUVWXYZ
MLKJGIHFEDCBA

in the alphabet?

The ones in the mail!

Red-knobbed hornbills are native to Sulawesi, an island in Indonesia, and other nearby islands.

104

Q Why did the cookie go to the hospital?

A Because it felt crummy.

Q **Why was 6 afraid of 7?**

A Because 7 8 9.

Q What has **four** legs but can't **walk?**

A A table.

Q Why do seagulls fly over the sea?

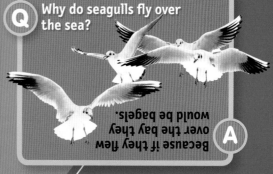

A Because if they flew over the bay they would be bagels.

105

Q How do you make a tissue dance?

A Put a little boogie in it!

Q What has **four eyes** but no **face?**

A Mississippi!

Q What do you call a **cheese** that is **not yours?**

A Nacho cheese.

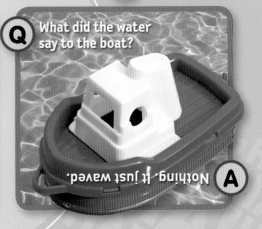

Q What did the water say to the boat?

A Nothing. It just waved.

106

What kind of **bow** can't be tied?

A rainbow!

What do you call an alligator that goes undercover?

Q

A

An investi-gator.

Koalas spend up to 18 hours a day napping.

Q

What can you serve but never eat?

A volleyball.

A

109

Seals mostly eat fish, squid, mollusks, and crustaceans.

111

Q What did one plate say to the other plate?

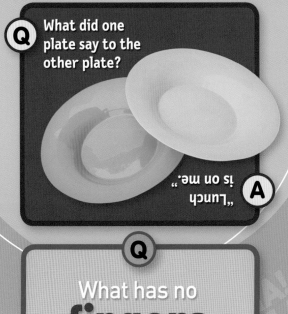

A "Lunch is on me."

Q What has no **fingers** but has many **rings?**

A A tree.

The llama is a South American relative of the camel.

KNOCK, KNOCK.

Who's there?
Botany.
Botany who?
Botany good books lately?

113

Smelly shoes and

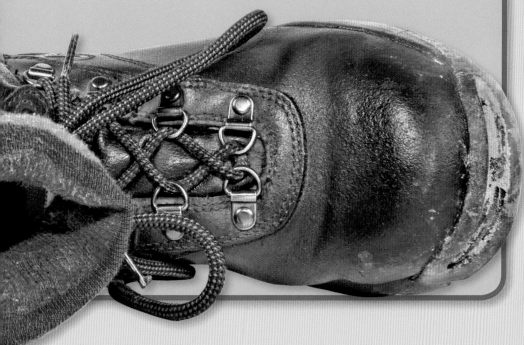

TONGUE TWISTER!

Say this fast three times:

socks shock Sis.

115

Male goats are called billies; female goats are called nannies.

KNOCK, KNOCK.

Who's there?
Clara.
Clara who?
Clara space at the table.

116

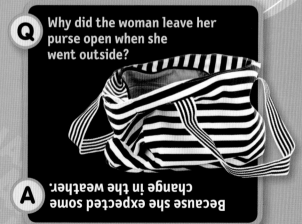

Q Why did the woman leave her purse open when she went outside?

A Because she expected some change in the weather.

117

TONGUE TWISTER!

Say this fast three times:

A glowing gleam glowing green.

Q What do you feed a noisy dog?

A Hush puppies.

Q What did the banana do when the monkey chased it?

A The banana split.

Q Why did the watchmaker enjoy his vacation?

A Because he learned to unwind.

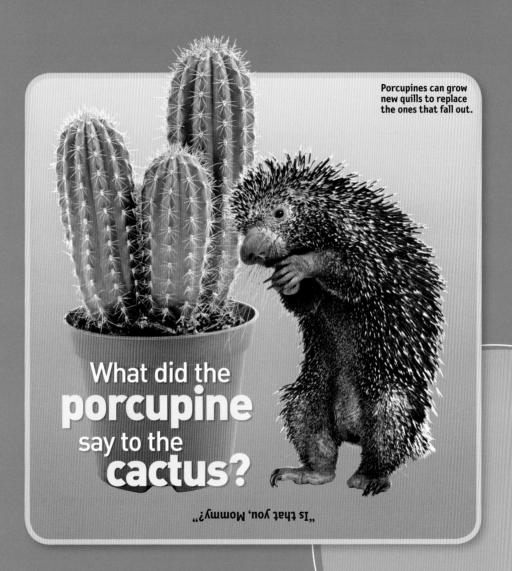

Porcupines can grow new quills to replace the ones that fall out.

What did the **porcupine** say to the **cactus?**

"Is that you, Mommy?"

119

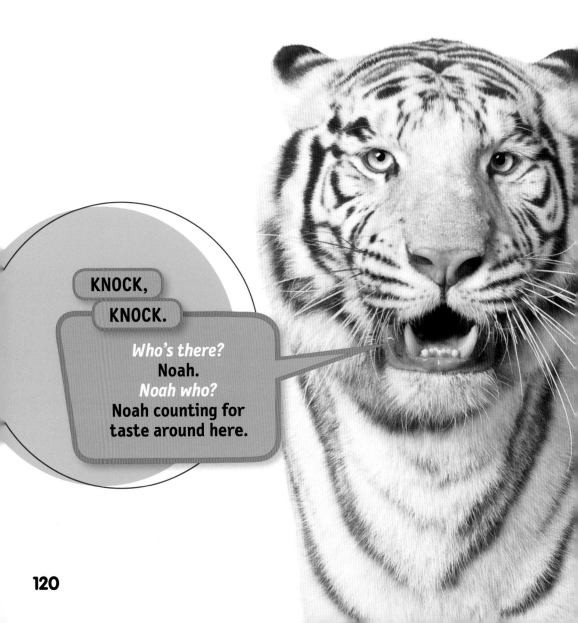

120

White tigers have
a rare gene that
changes the color
of their fur.

121

Guernsey cows like this one are bred for milk, not meat.

KNOCK, KNOCK.

Who's there?
Colleen.
Colleen who?
Colleen up this mess out here.

On the first day of class, the **teacher** asked all trouble-makers to stand up. After a few moments of silence, a **shy little girl** stood up. "Are you a troublemaker?" the teacher asked. "No," replied the girl. "I just hate to see you standing there **all by yourself**."

Q Why did the bowler move to the ocean?

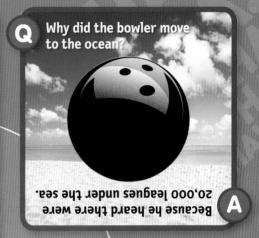

A Because he heard there were 20,000 leagues under the sea.

Q Why was the **fisherman** angry at the **computer?**

A He wasn't getting any bytes.

123

Q Which tree doesn't play checkers?

A The chess nut.

Q How many days of the week start with the letter *T*?

A Four. Tuesday, Thursday, today, and tomorrow.

January 2012

Sun	Mon	Tue	Wed	Thu	Fri	Sat
1	2	3	4	5	6	7
8	9	10	11	12	13	14
15	16	17	18	19	20	21
22	23	24	25	26	27	28
29	30	31				

TONGUE TWISTER!

Say this fast three times:

Fish sauce shop.

Q What goes snap, crackle, pop?

A A firefly with a short circuit.

Buy blue blueberry biscuits before bedtime.

There are more chickens on Earth than people.

What do you get if you cross a **chicken** with a **skunk?**

Skunk spray can travel as far as ten feet (3 m).

A fowl smell.

KNOCK, KNOCK.

Who's there?
Beets.
Beets who?
Beets me!

Sea otters float in groups of up to 100.

128

Q

Why couldn't the pirate play cards?

A Because he was sitting on the deck.

TONGUE TWISTER!

Say this fast three times:

Upper roller, lower roller.

PATIENT: Doctor, Doctor! I've lost my memory!
DOCTOR: When did this happen?
PATIENT: When did what happen?

Q Have you heard the rumor about the butter?

A I'd better not tell you. It might spread.

Q What do you do with a blue whale?

A  Try to cheer him up.

Tree squirrels are sometimes called "living fossils" because they look basically the same as they did five million years ago.

KNOCK,

KNOCK.

Who's there?
Tom Sawyer.
Tom Sawyer who?
Tom sawyer underpants.

131

A snail secretes liquid that hardens to form its shell.

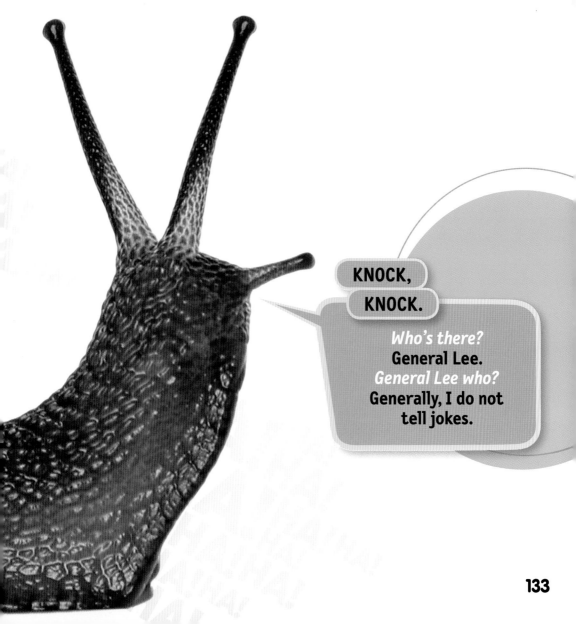

133

Ten toothsome tarts tempted Tom's tranquility.

Q Why did the barber win the race?

A Because he took a short cut.

Q Why was there thunder and lightning in the lab?

A Because the scientists were brainstorming.

Q What is **taken** before you get it?

A Your picture.

Q Why did it take the monster ten months to finish a book?

A He wasn't very hungry.

135

TONGUE
TWISTER!

Say this fast three times:

**Tie twine
to three tree
twigs.**

Q Why should you
take a **pencil**
to bed?

A To draw the curtains!

136

KNOCK,

KNOCK.

Who's there?
Dwayne.
Dwayne who?
Dwayne the bathtub,
I'm dwowning.

Red pandas live
in the trees in
mountain forests
of Asia.

137

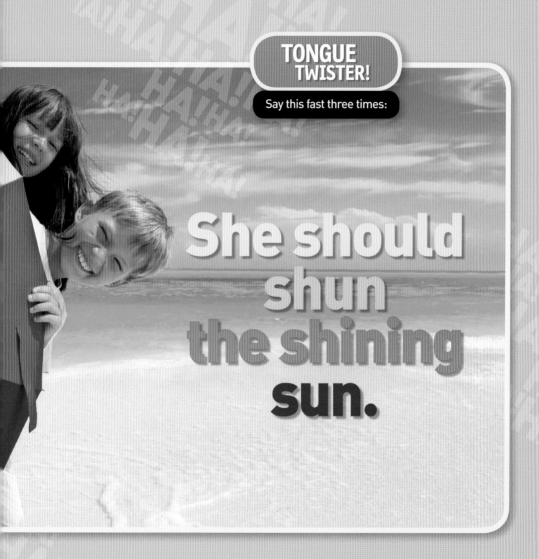

She should shun the shining sun.

Deer are native to all continents except Australia and Antarctica.

KNOCK, KNOCK.

Who's there?
Panther.
Panther who?
Panther what you wear on your legths.

140

Q What does a teddy bear put in his house?

A Fur-niture.

Q What season is it when you are on a trampoline?

A Spring time.

Q How many books can you put in an empty backpack?

A One! After that it's not empty.

Q What happens if you eat **yeast** and **shoe polish?**

A You'll rise and shine every morning.

141

Q

What **breaks** when you **say** it?

A Silence.

Q What do teenage geese suffer from?

A Goose pimples.

Q

What gets **bigger** the more you take away from it?

A A hole.

TONGUE TWISTER!

Say this fast three times:

Shave a single shingle thin.

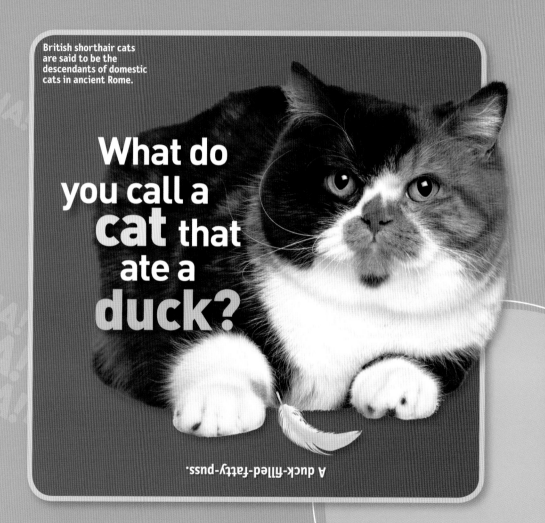

British shorthair cats are said to be the descendants of domestic cats in ancient Rome.

What do you call a **cat** that ate a **duck?**

A duck-filled-fatty-puss.

Female elephants are called cows.

144

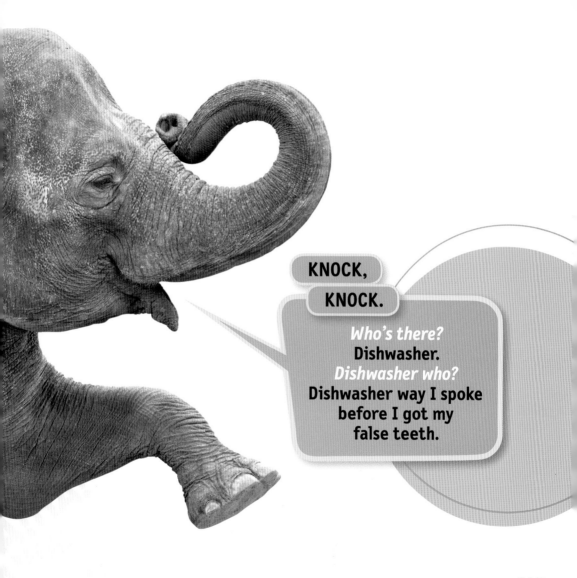

145

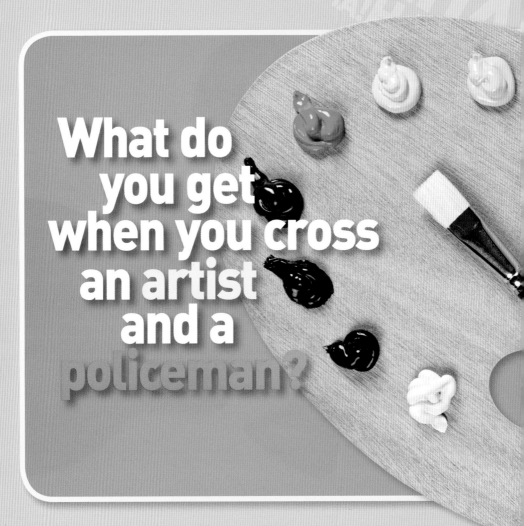

What do you get when you cross an artist and a policeman?

146

A brush with the law.

KNOCK, KNOCK.

Who's there?
Ketchup.
Ketchup who?
Ketchup with you soon!

148

Q

What did one elevator say to the other elevator?

A

"I think I'm coming down with something."

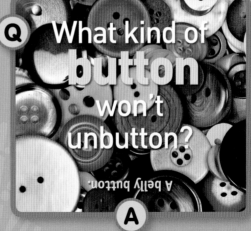

Q What kind of **button** won't unbutton?

A belly button.

A

149

Q Why did Tony go out with a prune?

A Because he couldn't find a date.

Q Why don't they serve **chocolate** in prison?

A Because it makes you break out.

Q Why did the man with one **hand** cross the road?

A To get to the second-hand shop.

TONGUE TWISTER!

Say this fast three times:

Bad money, mad bunny.

150

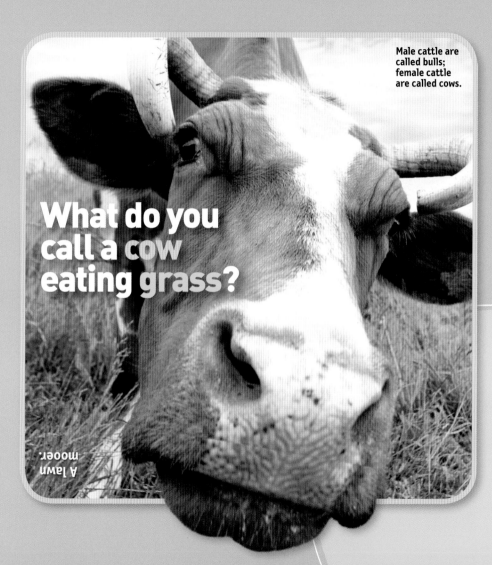

Male cattle are called bulls; female cattle are called cows.

What do you call a cow eating grass?

A lawn mooer.

Three gray geese in the green grass grazing.

A flock of geese is called a gaggle.

KNOCK, KNOCK.

Who's there?
Danielle.
Danielle who?
Danielle at me!
It's not my fault!

The male brown booby makes whistling sounds; the female quacks and honks.

154

Q Why did the little boy put lipstick on his head?

A He wanted to make up his mind.

Q Did you hear what happened at the Laundromat last night?

A Three clothespins held up two shirts.

155

Q What did the lamp say when it was turned off?

A "I'm delighted."

Q What gets **older** but doesn't age?

A A portrait.

Q Why did the boy study in the **airplane?**

A He wanted a higher education.

Q What flower grows on your face?

A Two-lips.

KNOCK, KNOCK.

Who's there?
Duncan.
Duncan who?
Duncan your dough-nut again?

Dromedary camels
like this one have
one hump; Bactrian
camels have two humps.

157

158

Brown bears
are often called
grizzlies because
of their grayish,
or grizzled fur.

What did the **baby corn** say to the **mother corn?**

"Where's pop-corn?"

Q What do you use to cut through giant waves?

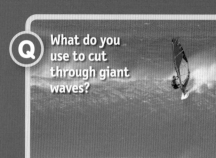

A A sea saw.

Q What kind of can never needs a can opener?

A A pelican.

Q How do you make an ant out of breath?

A Give it a p and make it pant.

Q What has a
neck
but cannot
swallow?

A A bottle.

161

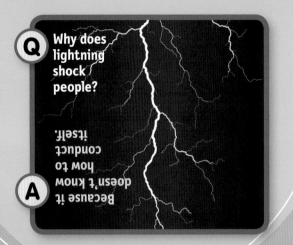

Q Why does lightning shock people?

A Because it doesn't know how to conduct itself.

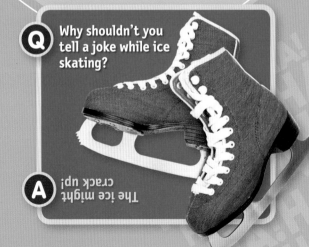

Q Why shouldn't you tell a joke while ice skating?

A The ice might crack up!

162

Female iguanas lay about 30 to 50 eggs at once.

KNOCK, KNOCK.

Who's there?
Canoe.
Canoe who?
Canoe lend me some money?

163

What is the difference between a **bottle of medicine** and a **doormat?**

One is shaken up and taken, and
the other is taken up and shaken.

165

Cheetahs only need to drink once every three to four days.

KNOCK, KNOCK.

Who's there?
Mara.
Mara who?
Mara, mara on the wall . . .

166

Say this fast three times:

The sixth sick sheikh's son slept.

Q What do you call seaside spooks?

A Ghost guards.

167

A horse's
wide-set eyes
allow it to
spot danger
more easily.

169

Q

What walks around with its **head** on the ground?

A A nail in a shoe.

Q Why did the birdie go to the hospital?

A To get a tweetment.

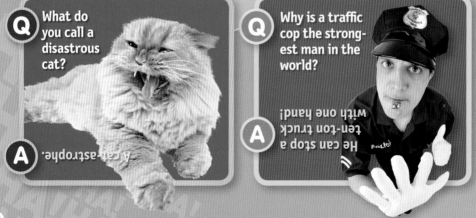

Q What do you call a disastrous cat?

A A cat-astrophe.

Q Why is a traffic cop the strongest man in the world?

A He can stop a ten-ton truck with one hand!

Why did
the boy
tiptoe
past the
**medicine
cabinet?**

He didn't want
to wake the
sleeping pills.

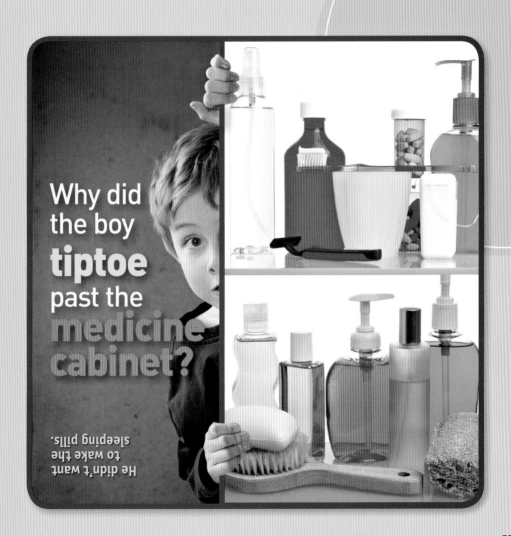

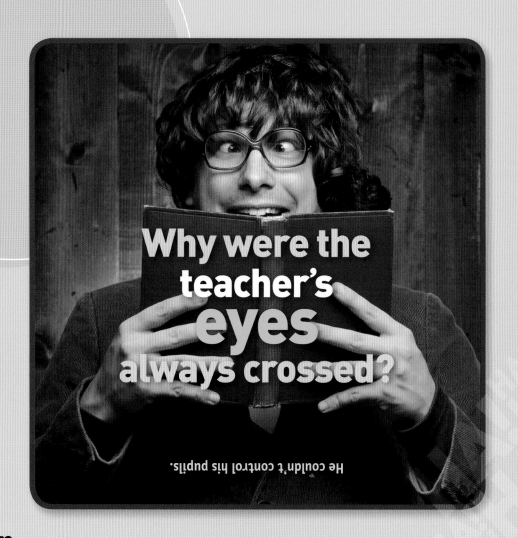

Why were the teacher's eyes always crossed?

He couldn't control his pupils.

Q When do you stop at green and go at red?

A When you're eating a watermelon.

Q Why was the broom late?

A It over swept.

Q What goes **up** when the rain comes **down?**

A An umbrella.

TONGUE TWISTER!

Say this fast three times:

Cinnamon aluminum linoleum.

Q What kind of cake do you get at the school cafeteria?

A A stomach-cake!

Q What **disappears** when you **stand up?**

A Your lap.

TONGUE TWISTER!

Say this fast three times:

Tragedy strategy.

Q What did the dog say to the flea?

A "You bug me!"

This ape is part chimpanzee, part bonobo.

KNOCK, KNOCK.

Who's there?
Formosa.
Formosa who?
Formosa the summer I was away on vacation.

175

Six sharp smart sharks.

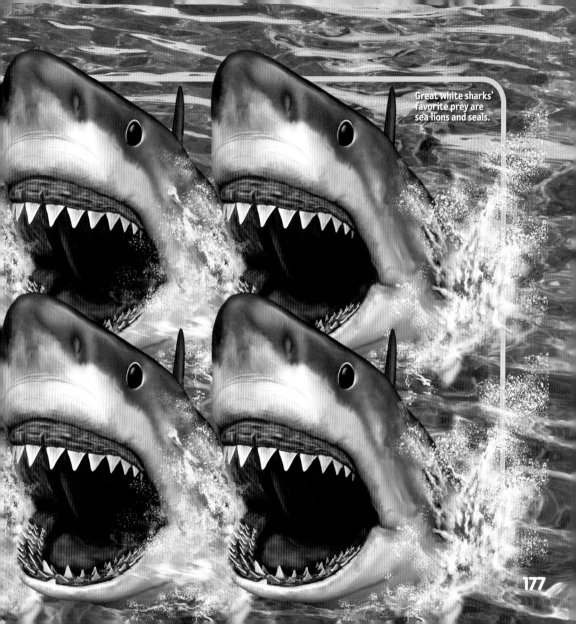

Great white sharks' favorite prey are sea lions and seals.

177

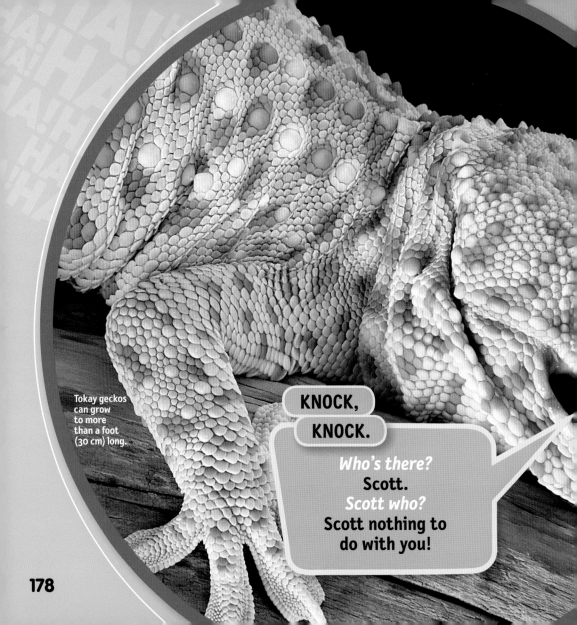

Tokay geckos can grow to more than a foot (30 cm) long.

178

Say this fast three times:

A bragging baker baked black bread.

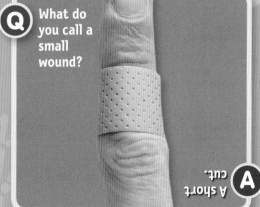

Q What do you call a small wound?

A A short cut.

179

A woman went to her psychiatrist and said, "Doctor, I want to talk to you about a problem. My husband thinks he's a refrigerator."

"Things could be worse," said the doctor. "That's a minor problem."

"It might be," replied the woman. "But he sleeps with his mouth open and the light keeps me awake!"

Say this fast three times:

Selfish shellfish.

Q

Why did the **computer** squeak?

Because someone stepped on its mouse.

A

Brown bears dig dens for winter hibernation.

KNOCK, KNOCK.

Who's there?
Robin.
Robin who?
Robin da bank!

181

182

If a goldfish is left in the dark for a long time, it will turn almost white.

Say this fast three times:

Preshrunk silk shirts.

Q

What gets smaller when you turn it upside down?

A The number 9.

Q What did the judge say when the skunk walked into the room?

A "Odor in the court."

Q What is the worst kind of driving school?

A The one that offers crash courses.

Q

What gets wetter the more that it dries?

A A towel.

185

Q Why didn't the skeleton go to the dance?

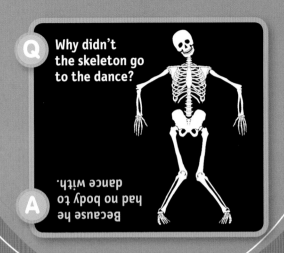

A Because he had no body to dance with.

Q Why did the turtle cross the road?

A To get to the Shell station.

Wolf guenon monkeys have cheek pouches to carry food as they travel.

KNOCK, KNOCK.

Who's there?
Usher.
Usher who?
Usher wish you would
let me in.

TONGUE TWISTER!

Say this fast three times:

This shop stocks

socks with spots.

189

KNOCK, KNOCK.

Who's there?
Vampire.
Vampire who?
Vampire State Building.

The beluga whale is one of the smallest species of whale.

190

Q Why can't your nose be 12 inches long?

A Because then it would be a foot!

Q Why did the boy sprinkle sugar on his pillow?

A So he could have sweet dreams.

Q When does a **cart** come **before** a **horse?**

A In the dictionary!

Q How do you know that carrots are good for your eyesight?

A Have you ever seen a rabbit wearing glasses?

Q

What is the **center** of gravity?

A The letter V.

Q Who are a hamburger's favorite people?

A Vegetarians.

Q What looks like half a tomato?

A The other half.

Q

Why did the **belt** go to jail?

A Because it held up a pair of pants.

Double-crested cormorants are strong swimmers and divers.

KNOCK, KNOCK.

Who's there?
Beezer.
Beezer who?
Beezer black and yellow and make honey.

193

KNOCK,
KNOCK.

Who's there?
Disguise.
Disguise who?
Disguise your
boyfriend.

A rabbit's
teeth never
stop growing.

Mountain goats are not true goats; they are actually goat-antelopes.

KNOCK, KNOCK.

Who's there?
Truffle.
Truffle who?
Truffle with you is that you're too shy!

196

Say this fast three times:

Thieves
seize
skis.

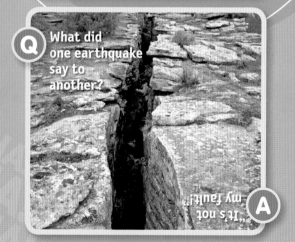

Q What did one earthquake say to another?

A "It's not my fault!"

197

Say this fast three times:

Sixish.

Q What do frogs drink?

A Croak-a-cola.

Q Why didn't the **hot dog** star in the **movies?**

A Because the rolls weren't good enough.

What did the big firecracker say to the little firecracker?

"My pop is bigger than yours."

199

Now **that** was funny!

JOKEFINDER

T

TONGUE TWISTERS

ILLUSTRATION CREDITS

National Geographic Kids would like to thank the following people for their invaluable expertise:

Robert Pascocello, *Scientific Assistant, Department of Herpetology, Division of Vertebrate Zoology, American Museum of Natural History*
Erin Stahler, *Biological Science Technician, Yellowstone Wolf Project*
Travis W. Taggart, *Director, Center for North American Herpetology*
Gaylene Thomas, *Animal Care Supervisor, San Diego Zoo*

Published by the National Geographic Society
John M. Fahey, Jr., *Chairman of the Board and Chief Executive Officer*
Timothy T. Kelly, *President*
Declan Moore, *Executive Vice President; President, Publishing and Digital Media*
Melina Gerosa Bellows, *Executive Vice President; Chief Creative Officer, Books, Kids, and Family*

Prepared by the Book Division
Hector Sierra, *Senior Vice President and General Manager*
Nancy Laties Feresten, *Senior Vice President, Kids Publishing and Media*
Jonathan Halling, *Design Director, Books and Children's Publishing*
Jay Sumner, *Director of Photography, Children's Publishing*
Jennifer Emmett, *Editorial Director, Children's Books*
Carl Mehler, *Director of Maps*
R. Gary Colbert, *Production Director*
Jennifer A. Thornton, *Director of Managing Editorial*

Based on the "Just Joking" department in
***National Geographic Kids* magazine**
Kelley Miller, *Senior Photo Editor*
Julide Dengel, *Designer*

Staff for This Book
Robin Terry, *Project Editor*
Eva Absher-Schantz, *Managing Art Director*
Lisa Jewell, *Photo Editor*
David M. Seager, *Art Director/Designer/Editor*
Grace Hill, *Associate Managing Editor*
Joan Gossett, *Production Editor*
Lewis R. Bassford, *Production Manager*
Susan Borke, *Legal and Business Affairs*
Kate Olesin, *Associate Editor*
Kathryn Robbins, *Design Production Assistant*
Hillary Moloney, *Illustrations Assistant*
Michaela Berkon, Molly Gasparre, Carly W. Larkin, *Editorial Interns*

Manufacturing and Quality Management
Phillip L. Schlosser, *Senior Vice President*
Chris Brown, *Vice President, Book Manufacturing*
George Bounelis, *Vice President, Book Production*
Nicole Elliott, *Manager*
Rachel Faulise, *Manager*
Robert L. Barr, *Manager*

Paperback ISBN: 978-1-4263-1016-4

Library ISBN: 978-1-4263-1017-1

Printed in China
14/PPS/2-BX

Just
Joking
3

NATIONAL GEOGRAPHIC
KIDS

Just Joking 3

300
hilarious jokes
about everything,
including
tongue twisters,
riddles,
and more!

by Ruth A. Musgrave

NATIONAL
GEOGRAPHIC
WASHINGTON, D.C.

KNOCK, KNOCK.

Who's there?
Alike.
Alike who?
Alike you,
you're funny!

Dogs' nose-
prints are
as unique
as human
fingerprints.

4

HA! HA! HA! HA! HA! HA! HA! HA! HA! HA! HA!

5

KNOCK, KNOCK.

Who's there?
Annie Mae.
Annie Mae who?
Annie Mae I have
a cookie?

6

Say this fast three times:

Chet cheated at checkers.

A black-tailed prairie dog greets other prairie dogs by clicking its front teeth together.

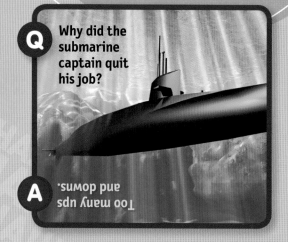

Q Why did the submarine captain quit his job?

A Too many ups and downs.

TONGUE TWISTER!

Say this fast three times:

Fifteen fumbling football players fell flat.

Q How do you stop a charging bull?

A Take away its credit cards.

Q How do you stop an octopus from punching you?

A Dis-arm it!

Q What's a boxer's favorite candy?

A Jawbreakers.

8

A harp seal pup grows a layer of blubber by nursing on its mother's high-fat milk.

KNOCK, KNOCK.

Who's there?
Detest.
Detest who?
Detest was so long I almost fell asleep.

9

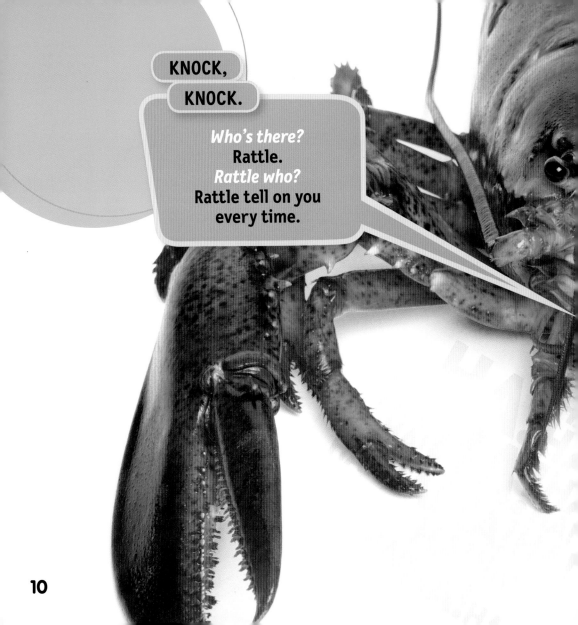

Live lobsters can be yellow, orange, brown, and even blue.

Q What did the TV say when its remote broke?

A "Help, I'm out of control!"

Q What do you get when you cross a charging rhino?

A Run over!

HA!HA!
HA!HA!
HA!HA!
HA!HA!
HA!HA!HA!

The spectacled caiman is named for the ridge that connects its eyes like a pair of spectacles, or glasses.

KNOCK, KNOCK.

Who's there?
Addle.
Addle who?
Addle be the last time I knock on your door.

13

Where do **aliens** stay in touch with their friends?

On Spacebook.

TONGUE TWISTER!

Say this fast three times:

Truly rural.

Q

Why didn't the **baseball player** score any points?

A He kept running home.

Q What does the Easter Bunny grow in his garden?

A Eggplants.

Q What's the Tower of Pisa's first name?

A Eileen.

TONGUE TWISTER!

Say this fast three times:

Top chopstick shops stock top chopsticks.

KNOCK,
KNOCK.

Who's there?
Ocelot.
Ocelot who?
Ocelot of pizza.
May I have a slice?

This African pit
viper's color—
attracts prey—
nectar-loving
birds that think
it's a flower.

18

Q **What do you call a** *cranky* *GPS?*

A A nag-ivator.

TONGUE TWISTER!

Say this fast three times:

Norse myths.

Q How do you make a moose float?

A Combine two scoops of ice cream, root beer, and one moose.

Q What is Kate's **clone's** name?

A Dupli-Kate.

Q Why was the bagel store easy to rob?

A Bad lox.

Q What's it called when you eat a banana sundae fast?

A Lickety split.

21

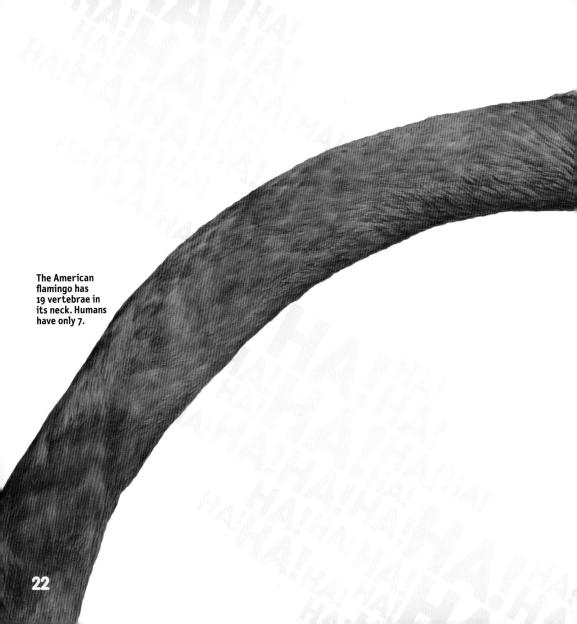

The American flamingo has 19 vertebrae in its neck. Humans have only 7.

22

23

Kangaroos can hop up to 25 feet (7.6 m). That's about as far as an Olympic long jumper can leap!

24

Q Why did the jellyfish run from every fight?

A It was spineless.

Q Where do **young tigers** swim?

In the kitty pool.

A

Q What's it called when a centipede trips?

A Scrambled legs.

Q Why did everyone think the big cat was lazy?

A Because he was always lion around.

25

Q What do you call the biggest onion ever found?

A A ton-ion.

Q What do you call twin monkeys hanging from a tree limb?

A A swing set.

Q Where do you **watch** people go up and down?

A A stare way.

Q What does a robin open at a picnic?

A A can of worms.

Bonobos sometimes chuckle when tickling each other or playing.

KNOCK, KNOCK.

Who's there?
Aiden.
Aiden who?
Aiden is where a fox lives.

27

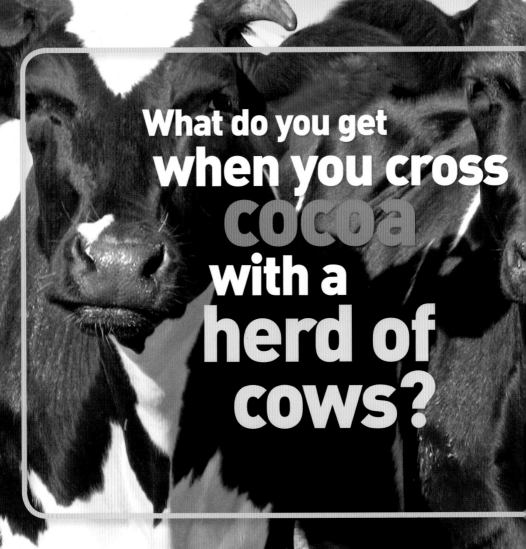

What do you get **when you cross** cocoa **with a** herd of cows?

Chocolate moos.

Tokay geckos use sticky hairlike structures on their toes to walk up walls.

KNOCK, KNOCK.

Who's there?
Two-thirds.
Two-thirds who?
Two-thirds, I need a dentist.

Q

What do apes like to eat with their milk?

A Chocolate chimp cookies.

Q Why did the girl toss a snail out the window?

A She wanted to see slime fly.

31

Q How do you stop a spamming spider?

A Kick it off the Web.

Q How can you tell when two mummies fall in love?

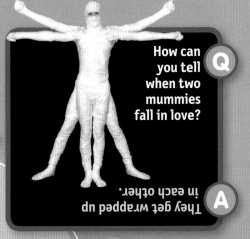

A They get wrapped up in each other.

Q Where should you never stop when snorkeling?

A A sharking lot.

Q What does a **cat** call a **mouse?**

A A squeak toy.

KNOCK,
KNOCK.

Who's there?
Hammond.
Hammond who?
Hammond eggs.

Badgers use their long claws to carve out burrows and dig for prey.

33

KNOCK, KNOCK.

Who's there?
Ascot.
Ascot who?
Ascot to go to the bathroom.

34

A giraffe's neck is about six feet long. That's as long as some humans are tall.

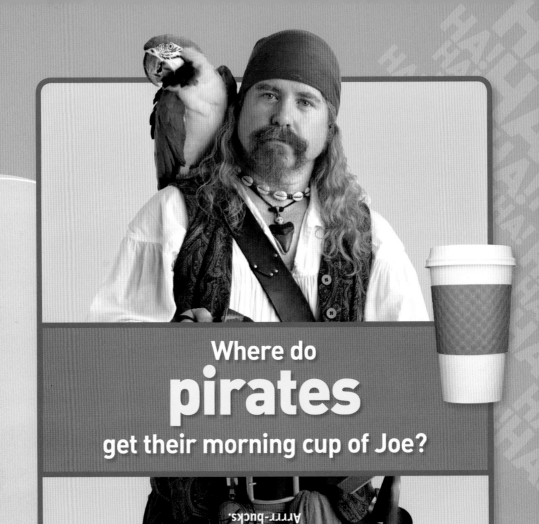

Where do
pirates
get their morning cup of Joe?

Arrr-bucks.

Q What does an octopus wear when it's cold?

A A coat of arms.

Q Why did the math whiz gain weight?

A Too much pi.

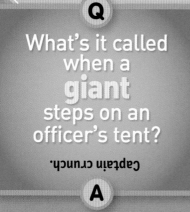

Q What's it called when a **giant** steps on an officer's tent?

A Captain crunch.

TONGUE TWISTER!

Say this fast three times:

Carl quietly quarters cucumbers.

Q What happened to the shark who swallowed a bunch of keys?

A He got lockjaw.

Hippos don't get sunburned because their sweat acts as sunblock.

Q What do Mickey Mouse and SpongeBob SquarePants listen to on the way to work?

Car tunes.

A

HA!HA! HA! HA! HA! HA! HA! HA! HA! HA! HA!HA! HA!HA! HA!HA!HA!

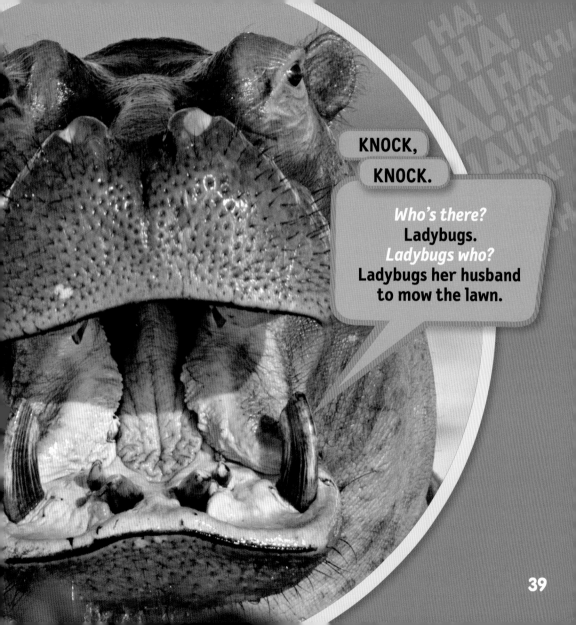

39

Ripe white reap ripe white

wheat reapers
wheat right.

41

The regal angelfish has a balloonlike bladder that helps it float.

What is the **best** way to **communicate** with a **fish?**

Drop it a line.

Q What does a penguin eat for breakfast?

A Ice crispies.

Q What do you do with an old bike?

A Re-cycle it.

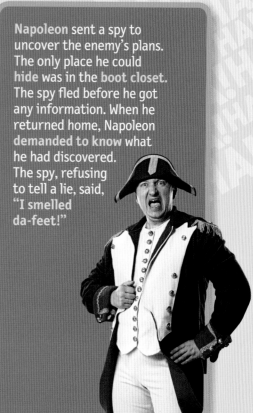

Napoleon sent a spy to uncover the enemy's plans. The only place he could hide was in the boot closet. The spy fled before he got any information. When he returned home, Napoleon demanded to know what he had discovered. The spy, refusing to tell a lie, said, "I smelled da-feet!"

French bulldogs originated in England, and later became popular in France.

KNOCK, KNOCK.

Who's there?
Alone.
Alone who?
Alone me a dollar?

44

Q What does it mean if you find a horse shoe?

A Some poor horse is walking around in his socks.

Q

What do you call it when a **cyclops** moves into a **frog's home?**

An eye-pad.

T. rex was about as long as a school bus!

46

47

Q Why did the dolphin quit the deep ocean choir?

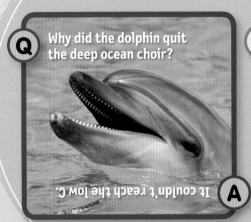

A It couldn't reach the low C.

Q Why did the baby bird get into trouble?

Tweet, Tweet, Tweet, Tweet, Tweet, Tweet, Tweet, Tweet, Tweet, Tweet, Tweet, Tweet, Tweet, Tweet.

A It sent too many tweets.

Q Why do **scouts** get stressed when they go **camping?**

A Because their lives are in tents.

Q Where do fish wash?

A In a river basin.

What do you get
when you cross a
giraffe
and a
maid?

Baby giraffes fall five feet to the ground when they are born.

I don't know, but my ceilings have never been so clean.

49

Q What do you call a doe caught in a storm?

A A rain deer.

Q What do you call a country where everyone has to drive a red car?

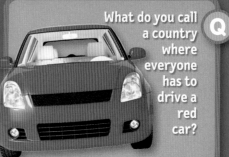

A A red car-nation.

Q What do you take before every meal?

A A seat.

Q

What can you hold without ever touching it?

A A conversation.

51

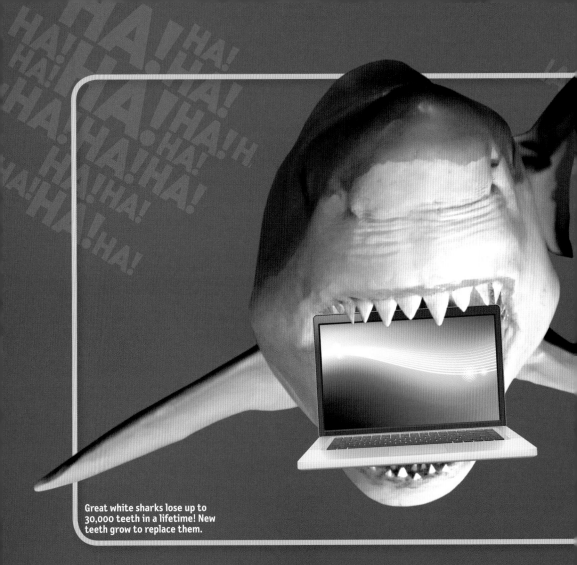

Great white sharks lose up to 30,000 teeth in a lifetime! New teeth grow to replace them.

What do you get when you cross a great white shark with a computer?

A mega-bite.

53

Margays sometimes mimic, or copy, the sounds of their prey.

KNOCK, KNOCK.

Who's there?
Anya.
Anya who?
Anya back is a hairy spider!

54

Q What does a bee use to cut wood?

A A buzz saw.

Q

Why did the
dog
cross the road
twice?

A He was trying to fetch a boomerang.

Q What does a surfer get when a big wave hits him in the face?

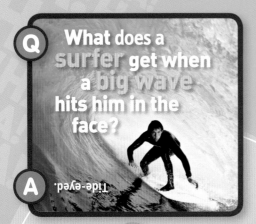

A Tide-eyed.

TONGUE TWISTER!

Say this fast three times:

Bog dogs blog.

Q Why did the scaredy cat cross the road?

A He was a real chicken.

Q Why wasn't the scarecrow ever invited to parties?

A He was a stuffed shirt.

56

What do you get
when you cross a
magician
and an oak?

Trick or tree.

57

58

If a poodle's coat isn't brushed, it forms ropelike chunks called cords.

59

The double-crested cormorant grows feather crests above its eyes when it is ready to mate.

60

Frank: One cow, two cows, three cows, four cows...

Hank: What are you doing?
Frank: I'm cownting.

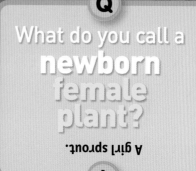

Q

What do you call a **newborn female plant?**

A girl sprout.

A

TONGUE TWISTER!

Say this fast three times:

Dueling dudes duel in the dew.

Q What does a lizard add when it remodels its kitchen?

A Reptiles.

61

Q What happens when you try to **sing** while **eating** a **deli sandwich?**

A You hum a tuna!

TONGUE TWISTER!

Say this fast three times:

Tickle the ticket taker.

Harp seal mothers can identify their pups by smell.

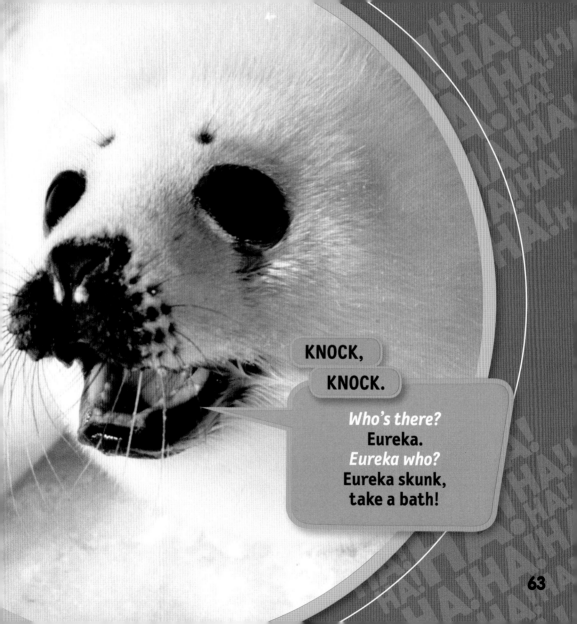

KNOCK, KNOCK.

Who's there?
Eureka.
Eureka who?
Eureka skunk,
take a bath!

63

What do you get
when you cross

a duck

and a

rooster?

I don't know, but it tastes fowl!

64

A rooster (above) has a rounded beak to grab seeds and insects. A mallard's flat beak (left) filters food from water.

The alpine marmot is considered the largest squirrel species.

KNOCK, KNOCK.

Who's there?
Tennis.
Tennis who?
Tennis a good time to meet.

Say this fast three times:

Shifting shark shadows shocked Sheila.

Q How do you make a clam shut up?

A Take away its shell phone.

67

Q

What did the **tree** wear to the pool party?

A

Swimming trunks.

KATHRYN: You said this cat was good for mice, but he never chases them.

EVA: Well, isn't that good for the mice?

Q How do you know if you've found a prehistoric treasure map?

A T. Rex marks the spot.

Q How do you know when a volcano gets mad?

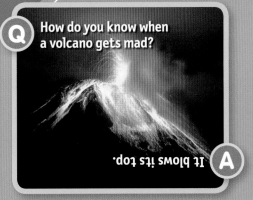

A It blows its top.

68

HA! HA! HA! HA!

In the wild, chimpanzees like to snack on termites.

Say this fast three times:

Chimp chomps chips.

69

KNOCK,
KNOCK.

Who's there?
Diggity.
Diggity who?
Diggity hole to
get to China.

Snow leopards
don't roar. They
often make a chuff,
or puffing sound,
when they show
aggression.

70

A wolf pack was chowing down on dinner. Suddenly, a pup fell over laughing. His mother looked at the rest of the pack and said, "He must have gotten the funny bone!"

How do you know a **zombie** is upset?

It falls to pieces.

Why did the kangaroo mother carry her change in her purse?

Her pocket was full.

71

Every tiger's
stripe pattern
is unique.

72

73

Q What is Cliff's coatrack called?

A A cliffhanger.

Q What do you call something that smells out of this **world?**

A Heaven scent.

TONGUE TWISTER!

Say this fast three times:

Will he really wheelie freely?

Q What do you name a feline that can't stand up straight?

A Catalina.

What kind of **medicine** does a **vampire** take when he has a **cold?**

Coffin syrup.

75

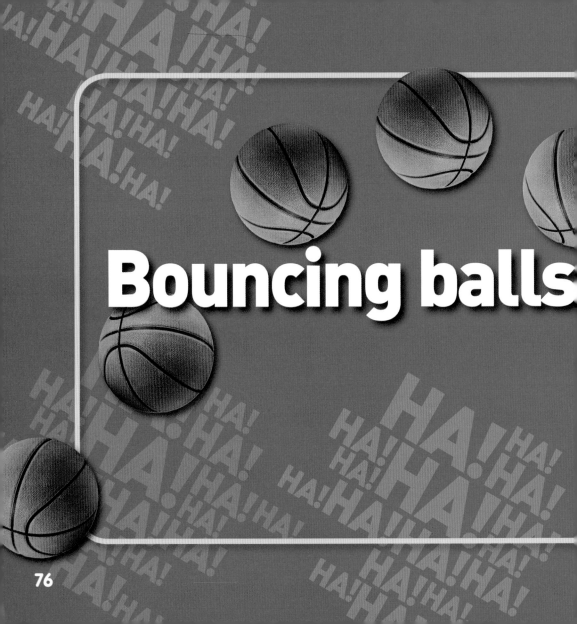

Bouncing balls

bounce off walls.

To keep cool in the desert, fennec foxes radiate body heat from their large ears.

KNOCK, KNOCK.

Who's there?
Ernest.
Ernest who?
Ernest is full of chicks.

78

Q What do you call a parasite that drives a dog crazy?

A A luna-tick.

TONGUE TWISTER!

Say this fast three times:

Sally slipped on snail slime.

Q What do you get when you cross a hamster and an automobile?

A A car-pet.

TONGUE TWISTER!

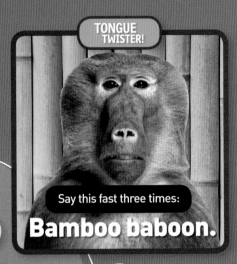

Say this fast three times:

Bamboo baboon.

TONGUE TWISTER!

Say this fast three times:

All aboard, bored boars.

Q What do you call a clumsy letter?

A A bumble B.

80

A zebra's teeth grow for its entire lifetime. The teeth are worn down by constant chewing and grazing.

KNOCK, KNOCK.

Who's there?
Surpass.
Surpass who?
Surpass the salt, please.

81

An elephant's trunk contains about 100,000 different muscles.

82

KNOCK,
KNOCK.

Who's there?
Snow.
Snow who?
Snow fun to clean
my room.

Swans' feathers trap body heat to keep them warm in cold climates.

KNOCK, KNOCK.

Who's there?
Statue.
Statue who?
Statue at the door?

84

Q

What's it called when a **mermaid** has to clean her room?

A sea chore.

A

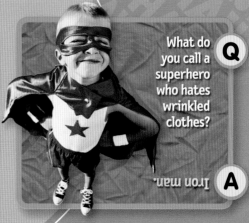

What do you call a superhero who hates wrinkled clothes?

Q

Iron man.

A

Q

What does an astronaut use to serve dinner?

A satellite dish.

A

Q

How did the rabbit win the wrestling match?

It used a hare pin.

A

85

Q What's it called when a jouster gets knocked off his horse?

A Knight fall.

Q What do you call a bird of prey who cries all the time?

A A bawling eagle.

HA! HA! HA! HA! HA! HA! HA! HA! HA!

86

The top of a loggerhead turtle's shell is heart-shaped.

KNOCK, KNOCK.

Who's there?
Water.
Water who?
Water you doing?

87

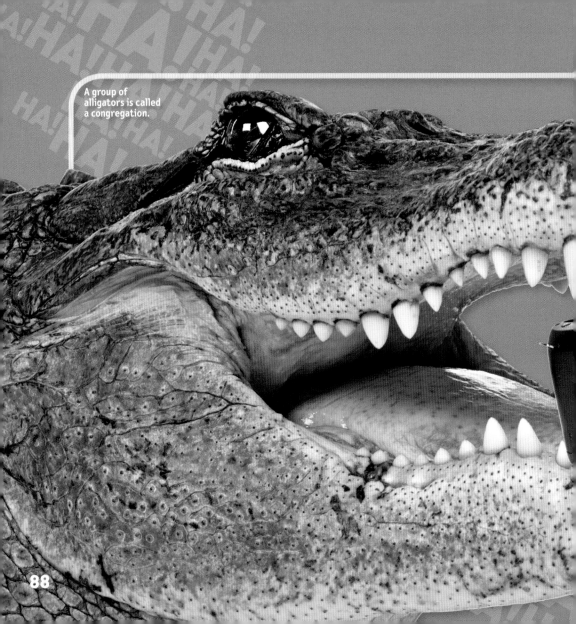

A group of
alligators is called
a congregation.

88

What kind of
photos do
alligators
take?

Snapshots.

89

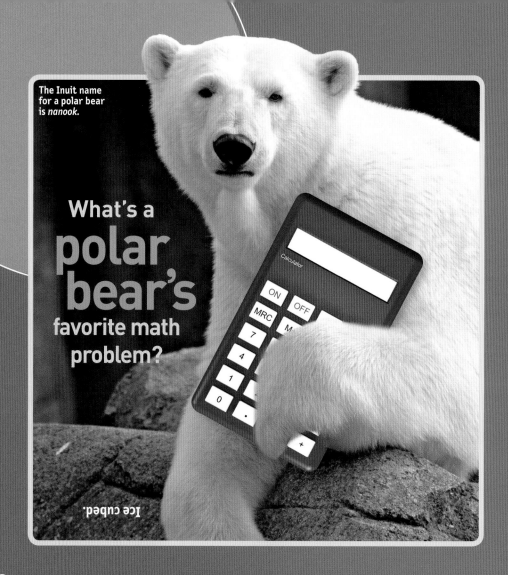

The Inuit name for a polar bear is *nanook*.

What's a
**polar
bear's**
favorite math
problem?

Ice cubed.

90

Q

What's it called when you are surrounded by **sharks?**

A A vicious circle.

Q What does a lawyer wear to work?

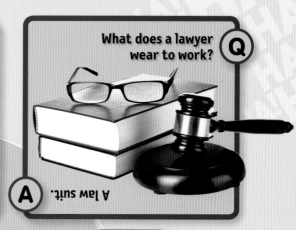

A A law suit.

Q What's a blizzard's favorite game?

A Freeze tag.

TONGUE TWISTER!

Say this fast three times:

A raccoon relaxed on racks of rackets.

BIG FLOWER:
What's up, Bud?

LITTLE FLOWER:
I'm busy blooming.

BIG FLOWER:
I'll leaf you alone.

Q

What do
boat captains
and
hat makers
worry about?

Capsizing.

A

Q

What do you get when you cross St. Nick with a crab?

Sandy claws.

A

What do you get when you cross a **curly dog** with a cinnamon cookie?

A snicker-poodle.

Poodles were originally bred to retrieve waterfowl for hunters.

93

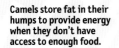

Camels store fat in their humps to provide energy when they don't have access to enough food.

KNOCK, KNOCK.

Who's there?
Adam's not.
Adam's not who?
Adam's not is dripping from his nose!

94

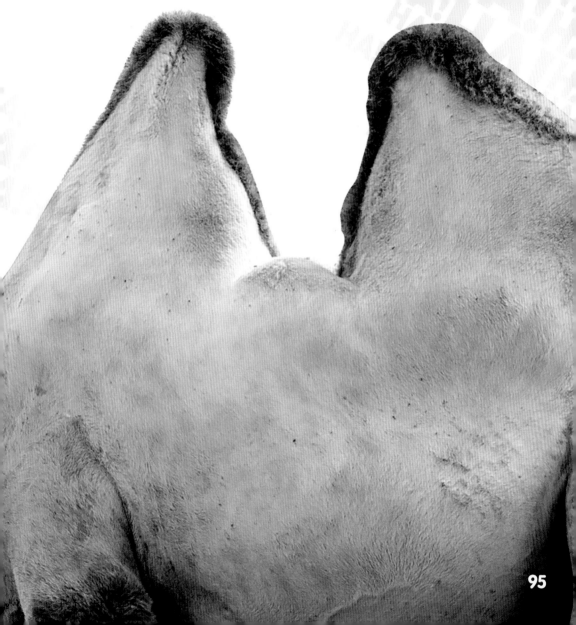

95

TONGUE TWISTER!

Say this fast three times:

Twelve toads

told tall tales.

Although most black bears are black, some are cinnamon-brown, silvery-blue, or white.

KNOCK, KNOCK.

Who's there?
Cattle.
Cattle who?
Cattle chase the mouse away.

98

Q What do you get when you cross ice cream with an angry ape?

A Grrrr-nilla.

Q

Why does the chef **laugh** when she cooks **breakfast?**

Because the egg always cracks a yolk.

A

99

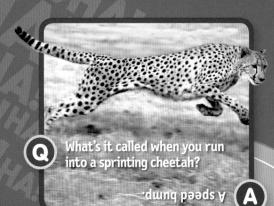

Q What's it called when you run into a sprinting cheetah?

A A speed bump.

Q Who does an insect call to repair its house?

A A carpenter ant.

Say this fast three times:

Gnats gnaw nuts.

Q What did the **guitar player** do to get his car out of the mud?

A He rocked and rolled it.

100

When threatened, the short-horned chameleon raises its earflaps to look larger.

KNOCK, KNOCK.

Who's there?
Popover.
Popover who?
Popover later for some ice cream.

101

What do you get when you cross popcorn,

POPCORN

102

a hot dog,
and
a
stack
of books?

Kernel Mustard in the library.

103

Geckos, including these leopard geckos, have the best eyesight of any lizard species studied.

KNOCK, KNOCK.

Who's there?
Marionette.
Marionette who?
Marionette the last piece of pie.

104

Q What do you get when you cross a tissue and a cook?

A A handker-chef.

Q What did the **police officers** do when they crashed their car into a bakery?

A They made copcakes.

Q Where do **twin leeches** go on the **Internet?**

A To a para-site.

Q What's a computer mouse's favorite snack?

A Microchips.

Q What do you get when you cross an ATM machine and a bovine?

A A cash cow.

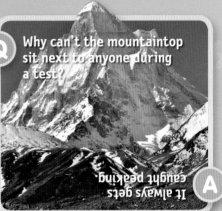

Q Why can't the mountaintop sit next to anyone during a test?

A It always gets caught peaking.

Q Why don't **Saturday** and **Sunday** ever get picked to play tug-of-war?

A Because they're always the weekend.

Q How does a reptile tune the radio?

A Croc-a-dials.

106

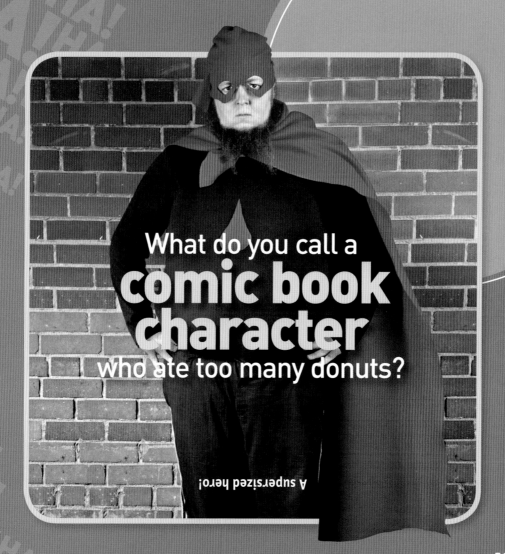

What do you call a
comic book
character
who ate too many donuts?

A supersized hero!

107

KNOCK, KNOCK.

Who's there?
Pickle.
Pickle who?
Pickle come in handy to get the lock open.

108

Q How do you write a letter on the ocean floor?

A Use sandpaper.

Q What's the **grumpiest** thing in your **yard?**

A Crab grass.

Koalas are often mistakenly called bears, but they are actually marsupials.

109

A pair of lovebirds will bond for life.

111

Q What did the stressed-out toad get?

A Worry warts.

Q What's a **sea monster's** favorite kind of sandwich?

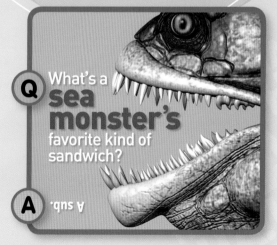

A A sub.

The red fox is the largest fox species.

112

113

Why didn't the boot believe the floor mat?

Because the mat lied like a rug.

114

115

A sheep may recognize the faces of other sheep in its herd.

KNOCK, KNOCK.

Who's there?
Acute.
Acute who?
Acute puppy wants you to come out and play.

116

TONGUE TWISTER!

Say this fast three times:

Cheap ship trip.

Q Where do minivans swim?

A In the carpool.

117

TONGUE TWISTER!

Say this fast three times:

Inchworms itching.

Q

What do you call **a rat** that gets run over **by a car?**

A road dent.

A

Q

Why did the **music students** get into trouble?

They were caught passing notes.

A

Q How did the pack animal get to the airport?

A It took a llama-sine.

HA! HA! HA! HA! HA! HA! HA!

What's the **funniest place** to wait for a soft drink **at a party?**

The punch line.

119

When the patriot crab buries itself in sand, it sticks out its eyestalks to see.

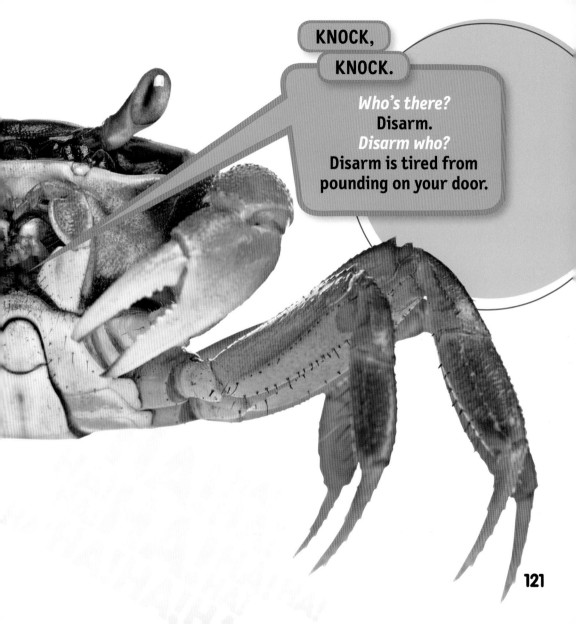

The emu's name comes from an old Arabic word that means "large bird."

KNOCK, KNOCK.

Who's there?
Stormy.
Stormy who?
Stormy skateboard in the garage, will ya?

GOLFER 1:
You better stay away from George today.

GOLFER 2:
Why?

GOLFER 1:
He's teed off.

Q What's it called when space rocks land on one side of the outfield?

A A meteor-right field.

Q

Why did the sci-fi fan wrap her car in **herbs?**

She loved thyme travel.

A

Q What happens when you leave the garbage outside in France?

A You get French flies.

Q Who do you call for underwater repairs?

A A sawfish and a hammerhead.

Q Where does a dog go to get a new tail?

A A retail store.

Q What kind of ring does a fry cook give his girlfriend?

A An onion ring.

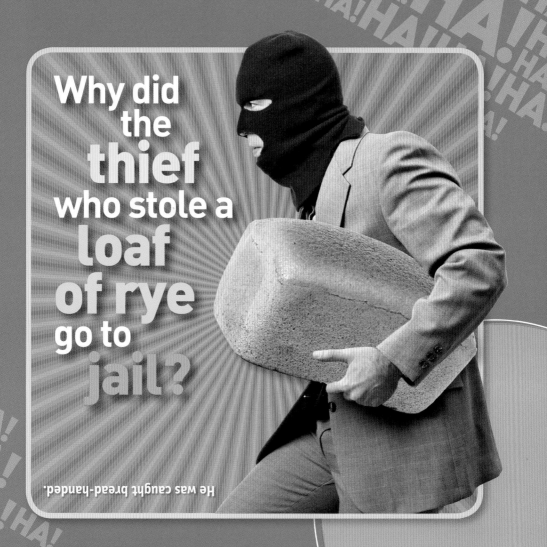

Why did
the
thief
who stole a
loaf
of rye
go to
jail?

He was caught bread-handed.

125

What's it called when you **remove half the rabbits**

from a **field?**

A harecut.

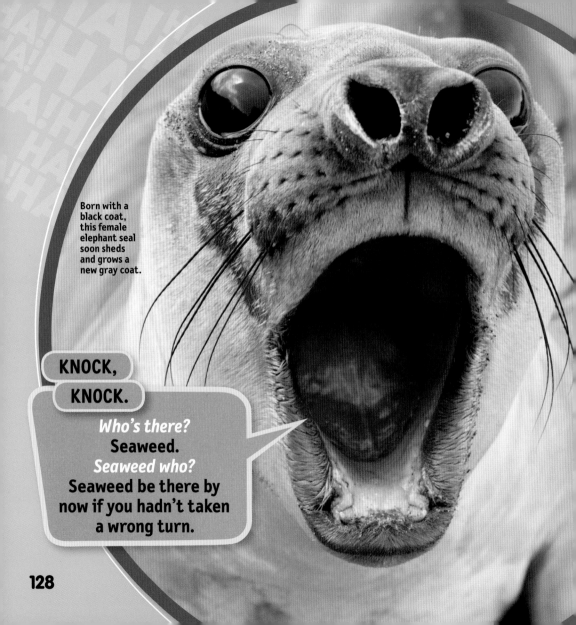

Born with a black coat, this female elephant seal soon sheds and grows a new gray coat.

KNOCK, KNOCK.

Who's there?
Seaweed.
Seaweed who?
Seaweed be there by now if you hadn't taken a wrong turn.

128

Q Why couldn't the lock sleep?

A It was all keyed up.

TONGUE TWISTER!

Say this fast three times:

Greek grapes.

129

TEACHER: Don't you dare tell me the dog ate your homework!

JEREMY: Nah, that excuse is so old, my grandpa used it.

TEACHER: Good. Now, where's your homework?

JEREMY: I don't have it, my mouse took too many bytes out of it.

Q What do you call an unlucky psychic?

A An unfortunate teller.

Q Why did the beekeeper quit his job?

A He kept getting hives.

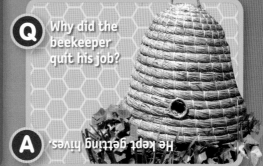

HA!HA!HA!HA!HA!HA!HA!

130

A swamp rabbit sometimes hides from predators underwater, keeping only its nose above water to breathe.

KNOCK, KNOCK.

Who's there?
Kayak.
Kayak who?
Kayak with you about something?

131

Tree frogs have sticky disks on their fingers and toes that help them climb on leaves.

KNOCK, KNOCK.

Who's there?
Mummify.
Mummify who?
Mummify clean my room,
may I go to the mall?

133

Say this fast three times:

24-70mm 1:2.8

Ø77mm

Camille's camera captured a camouflaged camel.

Q Why was the dough happy?

A Because everyone kneaded him.

Q Why did the soup never tell a joke?

A It didn't want to be a laughing-stock.

Q Why was the **calendar** so jumpy?

A It was a leap year.

Q Why did the stegosaurus need a bandage?

A He had a dino sore.

TONGUE TWISTER!

Say this fast three times:

Alice asks for axes.

Oriental small-clawed otters use at least a dozen calls to communicate.

Q Why was the strawberry in trouble?

A It was always in a jam.

HA! HA! HA! HA! HA! HA! HA! HA! HA! HA!

KNOCK, KNOCK.

Who's there?
Target.
Target who?
Target on your shoe, and now you're stuck to the floor.

137

What do you get when you cross a fish and a judge?

The scales of justice.

KNOCK,

KNOCK.

Who's there?
Leasing.
Leasing who?
Leasings off-key.

The great gray owl dives headfirst into the snow to catch voles, mouselike rodents that burrow in the snow.

140

Q Why did the bike appear on television?

A It was a good spokesperson.

Q Why was the worm found guilty of robbery?

A It didn't have a leg to stand on.

Q Where do cheeseburgers get to know each other?

A At a meat and greet.

Q What **text message** would you get from a **hyena?**

A lol.

141

Q When is traffic like an infant?

A When it crawls.

Q What did the boy say when he was accused of tying his dad's shoelaces together?

A Knot true.

Q Where do cats wait to pay their bills?

A The fee line.

TONGUE TWISTER!

Say this fast three times:

Much-mashed mushrooms.

What made the
deck of cards
disappear?

It got lost in the shuffle.

Elephants sometimes entwine their trunks to greet each other.

144

145

Did you hear about the little birds that started an airline?

They had cheep flights.

147

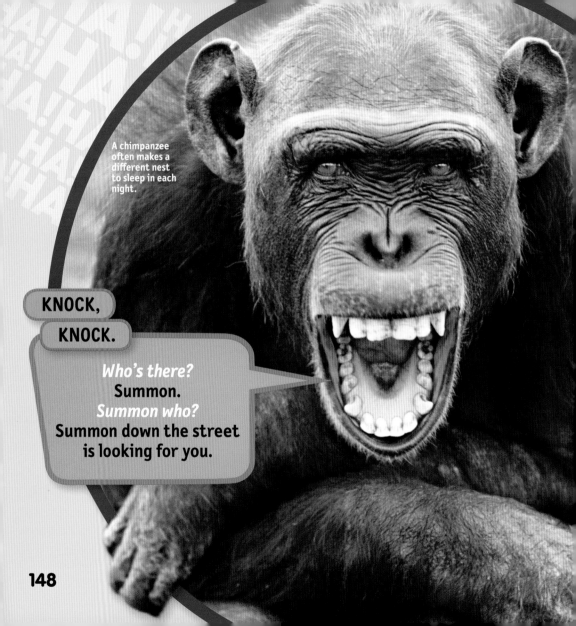

A chimpanzee often makes a different nest to sleep in each night.

KNOCK, KNOCK.

Who's there?
Summon.
Summon who?
Summon down the street is looking for you.

148

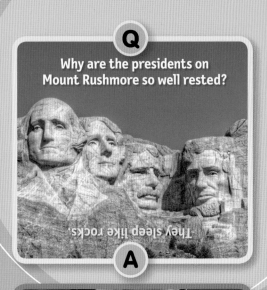

Q

Why are the presidents on Mount Rushmore so well rested?

A

They sleep like rocks.

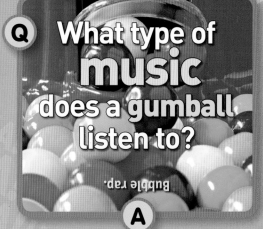

Q What type of **music** does a gumball listen to?

A

Bubble rap.

Q What does a firefly order at a restaurant?

A A light meal.

Q Why did the **patient** with **amnesia** go for a **run?**

A To jog her memory.

Q What do **puzzles** say when they **fight?**

A Crosswords.

TONGUE TWISTER!

Say this fast three times:

Ted texts Tess in Texas.

How does a ghost lock its door?

With a dead bolt.

Friendly Frank flips fine flapjacks.

153

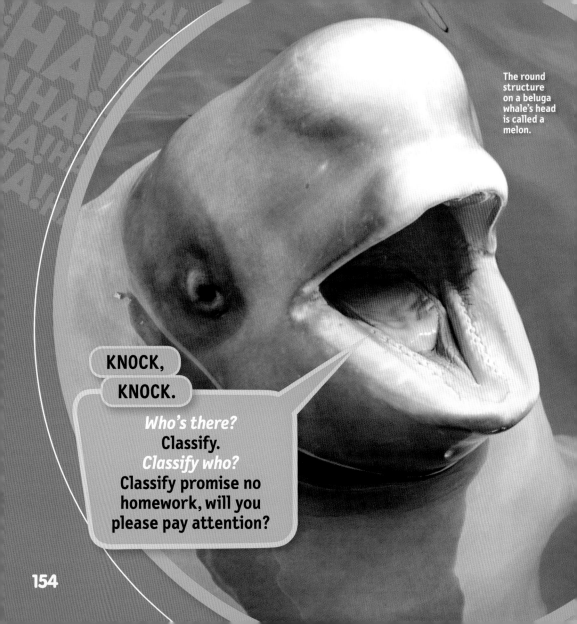

The round structure on a beluga whale's head is called a melon.

154

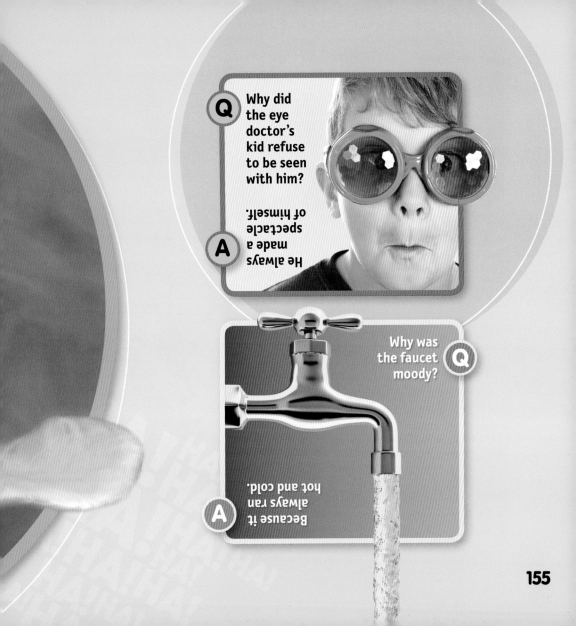

Q Why did the eye doctor's kid refuse to be seen with him?

A He always made a spectacle of himself.

Q Why was the faucet moody?

A Because it always ran hot and cold.

155

Q Why was the orange afraid of the mobsters?

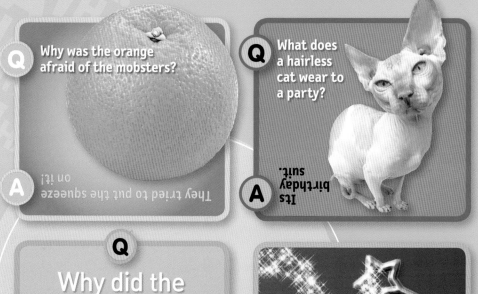

A They tried to put the squeeze on it!

Q What does a hairless cat wear to a party?

A Its birthday suit.

Q Why did the **muffler** quit the **car business?**

A It was exhausted.

Q What do you call a fairy godmother who can't make decisions?

A Wishy-washy.

KNOCK, KNOCK.

Who's there?
Distaste.
Distaste who?
Distaste
terrible!

A dusky leaf monkey utters a loud call to say, "Get off my turf!"

157

KNOCK, KNOCK.

Who's there?
Trainee.
Trainee who?
Trainee was trying to catch left ten minutes ago.

158

Lion cubs are
born blind.
They begin to
see when they
are about one
week old.

159

Eleven lemons.

Q Why didn't anyone trust the salmon?

A They smelled something fishy.

Q What do you call your shoes when you walk on ice?

A Slippers

Q Why did everyone avoid talking to the cook at the barbecue restaurant?

A She was always grilling people

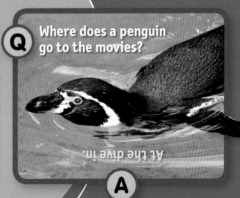

Q Where does a penguin go to the movies?

A At the dive in.

Q Why do astronauts look forward to liftoff?

A Because it's always a blast!

Q What's it called when a dog runs a long way to retrieve a ball?

A Far-fetched.

Domestic pigs—usually raised on farms—have curly tails. Wild pigs have straight tails.

KNOCK, KNOCK.

Who's there?
Internet.
Internet who?
Internet is where the basketball goes.

163

If two witches were watching two watches, which witch would watch which watch?

Elephant seals are named for the trunklike snout that extends from the male's head.

166

Say this fast three times:

Seven
Sasquatches
squashed
Sasha.

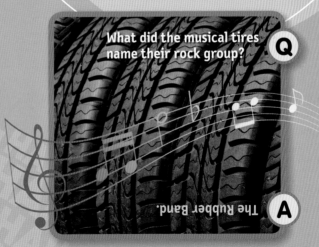

Q What did the musical tires name their rock group?

A The Rubber Band.

The Chinese name for panda is *daxiongmao*, which means "large bear-cat."

168

169

Q

What instrument does **Dumbo** play?

A

An eardrum.

Q Why was the grizzly turned away from the restaurant?

A No bear feet allowed.

Q Who keeps putting beards on dogs?

A The Dog Whiskerer.

Q Why didn't the veterinarian want to treat the toad?

A She was afraid it would croak.

170

Why did the **android** remove his **hard drive?**

Because he wanted to change his mind.

Why did the **socks** move to the orchard?

They liked living in pairs.

Q

How do you know when water gets mad?

A It sits and steams.

Q

What always has its hands in front of its face?

A A clock.

Q

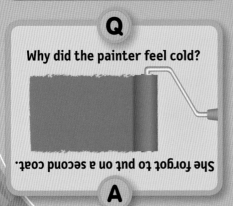

Why did the painter feel cold?

She forgot to put on a second coat. **A**

TONGUE TWISTER!

Say this fast three times:

Rough Ralph raffled ruffles.

173

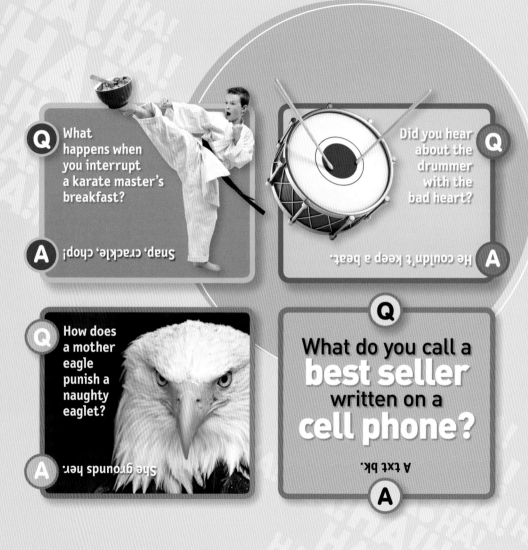

Q What happens when you interrupt a karate master's breakfast?

A Snap, crackle, chop!

Q Did you hear about the drummer with the bad heart?

A He couldn't keep a beat.

Q How does a mother eagle punish a naughty eaglet?

A She grounds her.

Q What do you call a **best seller** written on a **cell phone?**

A A txt bk.

Spoonbills use their spoon-shaped beaks to snatch up fish and other small aquatic creatures.

175

Why did the **mop** sign up for a self-defense class?

Because everyone tried to wipe the floor with it.

177

Red pandas like to sleep with their tails wrapped around their heads.

KNOCK, KNOCK.

Who's there?
Aboard.
Aboard who?
Aboard is missing from your front porch.

178

Q What does a Martian call his patio?

A Outer space.

Q Why did the man's bed disappear?

A It went undercover.

179

Q How did the door react to bad news?

A It became unhinged.

DETECTIVE: Rover, you're the one who's been tearing up the neighbor's shoes!

ROVER: How did you catch me?

DETECTIVE: If the chew fits...

TONGUE TWISTER!

Say this fast three times:

I love unique New York.

Female iguanas are attracted to males with long, healthy spines on their backs.

KNOCK, KNOCK.

Who's there?
Wafer.
Wafer who?
Wafer me, I'm almost ready.

181

182

A group of capuchins is called a barrel of monkeys or a troop.

Say this fast three times:

The two-toed tree toad tried to tread where the three-toed tree toad trod.

Q

Why did the man buy
plane tickets
for a bunch of
hogs?

A His boss said he could have a raise when pigs fly.

Q Why did the cold cuts refuse to be in a sandwich with the slice of bread?

A The bread was a real heel.

Q Where can you dig up a good joke?

A On a funny farm.

Q Why did the boy think he was psychic when he found change in his pocket?

A Because he discovered that he had six cents.

185

Q What did the snowman do when he got mad?

A He had a meltdown.

Q What did the cranky man say to the flower vendor?

A Go petal your stuff somewhere else.

186

This is a zither.

A zither is a stringed instrument that a musician often plays while holding the instrument in his lap.

189

Like all reptiles, this sand lizard can't produce its own body heat. It basks in the sun to keep warm.

KNOCK, KNOCK.

Who's there?
Shhh.
Shhh who?
Stop shooing me away!
That's rude.

190

Q Why was the cliff such a great poker player?

A It knew how to bluff.

Q What's the friendliest thing in a parade?

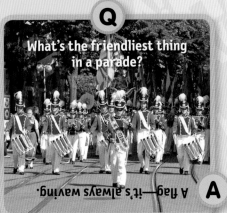

A A flag—it's always waving.

Q Why was the **cemetery** **owner** so **paranoid?** He saw plots everywhere!

A

Q Why did the mallard stick its head under the water?

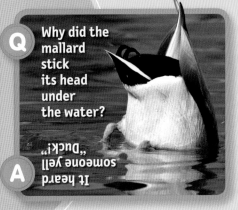

A It heard someone yell "Duck!"

Q

How did the **cat** get a **drink** from the Milky Way?

A It used the Big Dipper.

Q Why did the library have to be fumigated?

A It was full of bookworms.

Q Why were the computers afraid of the guy with a bad cold?

A He was always hacking.

Q

What do you call a **pretty woman** who flees from a **fashion show?**

A A runaway model.

The shoebill is named for its large beak, which is shaped like a pointy shoe.

KNOCK, KNOCK.

Who's there?
Ahead.
Ahead who?
Ahead of a monster just peaked over your shoulder.

193

A rhinoceros's horn and human fingernails are made from similar substances.

194

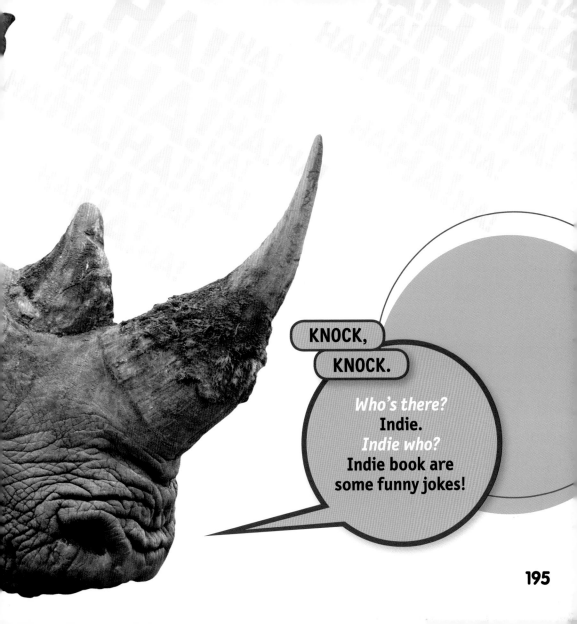

195

The oldest male lions in a pride often have the darkest manes.

KNOCK, KNOCK.

Who's there?
Samurai.
Samurai who?
Samurai will pick you up in an hour.

196

Q

Why was the bandleader not allowed to drive a train?

A He was a bad conductor.

TONGUE
TWISTER!

Say this fast three times:

Jack's knapsack strap snapped.

197

Say this fast three times:

Six thick thistle sticks.

Q Where do cardboard cartons fight each other?

A In a boxing ring.

Q What does an **artist** use to hold up his **pants?**

A A drawstring.

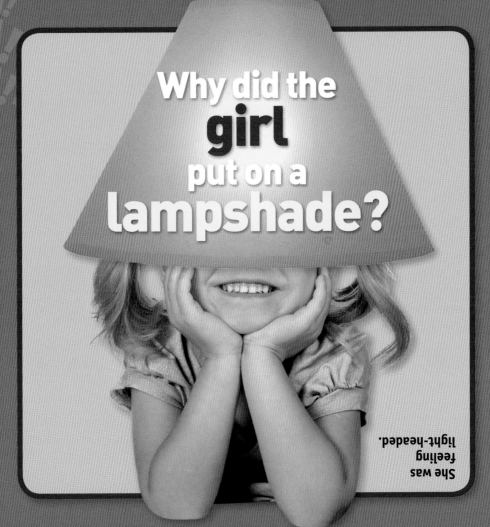

Why did the **girl** put on a **lampshade?**

She was feeling light-headed.

199

Otters close their eyes
and nostrils when they
dive underwater.

201

JOKEFINDER

203

ILLUSTRATION CREDITS

207

Published by the National Geographic Society

John M. Fahey, Jr., *Chairman of the Board and Chief Executive Officer*
Timothy T. Kelly, *President*
Declan Moore, *Executive Vice President; President, Publishing*
Melina Gerosa Bellows, *Executive Vice President; Chief Creative Officer, Books, Kids, and Family*

Prepared by the Book Division

Hector Sierra, *Senior Vice President and General Manager*
Nancy Laties Feresten, *Senior Vice President, Kids Publishing and Media*
Jonathan Halling, *Design Director, Books and Children's Publishing*
Jay Sumner, *Director of Photography, Children's Publishing*
Jennifer Emmett, *Vice President, Editorial Director, Children's Books*
Eva Absher-Schantz, *Design Director, Kids Publishing and Media*
Carl Mehler, *Director of Maps*
R. Gary Colbert, *Production Director*
Jennifer A. Thornton, *Director of Managing Editorial*

Staff for This Book

Robin Terry, *Project Editor*
David M. Seager, *Art Director*
Lisa Jewell, *Illustrations Editor*
Ruthie Thompson, *Designer*
Nancy Honovich, *Researcher*
Kate Olesin, *Associate Editor*
Kathryn Robbins, *Associate Designer*
Hillary Moloney, *Illustrations Assistant*
Grace Hill, *Associate Managing Editor*
Joan Gossett, *Production Editor*
Lewis R. Bassford, *Production Manager*
Susan Borke, *Legal and Business Affairs*

Manufacturing and Quality Management

Phillip L. Schlosser, *Senior Vice President*
Chris Brown, *Vice President, NG Book Manufacturing*
George Bounelis, *Vice President, Production Services*
Nicole Elliott, *Manager*
Rachel Faulise, *Manager*
Robert L. Barr, *Manager*

Based on the "Just Joking" department in
National Geographic Kids magazine

CELEBRATING
‹125›
YEARS

The National Geographic Society is one of the world's largest nonprofit scientific and educational organizations. Founded in 1888 to "increase and diffuse geographic knowledge," the Society works to inspire people to care about the planet. National Geographic reflects the world through its magazines, television programs, films, music and radio, books, DVDs, maps, exhibitions, live events, school publishing programs, interactive media and merchandise. *National Geographic* magazine, the Society's official journal, published in English and 33 local-language editions, is read by more than 38 million people each month. The National Geographic Channel reaches 320 million households in 34 languages in 166 countries. National Geographic Digital Media receives more than 15 million visitors a month. National Geographic has funded more than 9,400 scientific research, conservation and exploration projects and supports an education program promoting geography literacy. For more information, visit nationalgeographic.com.

For more information, please call 1-800-NGS LINE (647-5463)
or write to the following address:
National Geographic Society
1145 17th Street N.W.
Washington, D.C. 20036-4688 U.S.A.

Visit us online at nationalgeographic.com/books

For librarians and teachers: ngchildrensbooks.org

More for kids from National Geographic: kids.nationalgeographic.com

For information about special discounts for bulk purchases, please contact National Geographic Books Special Sales: ngspecsales@ngs.org

For rights or permissions inquiries, please contact National Geographic Books Subsidiary Rights: ngbookrights@ngs.org

Library of Congress Cataloging-in-Publication Data

Just joking 3: 300 hilarious jokes about everything, including tongue twisters, riddles, and more! / National Geographic Society.
    p. cm.
  Includes index.
  ISBN 978-1-4263-1098-0 (pbk. : alk. paper) -- ISBN 978-1-4263-1099-7 (library binding : alk. paper)
  1. Wit and humor, Juvenile. I. National Geographic Society (U.S.)
  PN6166.J663 2013
  818'.60208--dc23
                              2012026528

Printed in China

14/PPS/2